D0250627

Munich Memoir

Dan Alon's Untold Story of Survival

by Dan Alon, as told to Carla Stockton

Published and distributed by Dapt'd.

www.daptd.com

info@daptd.com

Cover design & layout by Edward Ludvigsen

©2012 Dan Alon

Photos used within the book are from the personal collection of Dan Alon, and are used with permission.

Additional photos by Zelig Struch, used with permission.

Back cover photo of Dan Alon used with the kind permission of Gert Krautbauer. Photo ©2012 Gert Krautbauer. All rights reserved. www.krautbauer.net

All rights reserved. No part of this book may be reproduced in any form or by any means without permission in writing from the publisher, except for the inclusion of brief quotations in a review.

ISBN 978-0-9856436-0-7

Table of Contents

Acknowledgements 8

Introduction 11

Chapter 1, Memory 13
Chapter 2, Time Stands Still in Heaven and Hell 20
Chapter 3, Aftermath 68
Chapter 4, In My Father's Court 87
Chapter 5, Winning the Title/Winning the Girl 105
Chapter 6, Yahrzeit: Yom Kippur War 118
Chapter 7, Approaching Xanadu 126
Chapter 8: Collision of Dreams 138
Chapter 9: Living By The Sword: A Brief and Personal
Look at Fencing and Its History 145
Chapter 10, The Swordsman In Me 168
Chapter 11, Peace In Our Time - Life Goes On 174
Chapter 12, Finding My Voice 180
Chapter 13, Relearning To Breathe 187
Chapter 14, Epilogue: Reunion 191

Afterword 199

Acknowledgements

I wish to acknowledge the Chabad Lubavitch Organization for their enormous contribution to my recovery, to my determination to tell my story and to my re-commitment to life. The organization itself is one that tirelessly works to ensure that each generation knows the stories that keep the Jewish faith alive. Born in the city of Lubavitch, Russia, whose name means the City of Brotherly Love, Chabad is an acronym composed of three Hebrew words meaning wisdom, comprehension and knowledge. The organization represents a deep and abiding love for all the world's Jewry, and they champion Jewish history as well as the continuation of Judaism through education and outreach programs directed at their own co-religionists. They foster good will among their gentile neighbors in every community and seek only to bring Jews back to Judaism through gentle good works.

I am grateful to Rabbi Eli Brackman for having encouraged me first in London; but my most eternal gratitude goes to Rabbi Shua Rosenstein, at Yale, who has made it his noble mission to ensure that people know what happened in Munich, that people understand the deep significance of the Munich Massacre and what it portends for our present and future generations.

I am humbled by the courage and the sacrifice of my fallen comrades, and I thank each of their surviving loved ones for carrying on, for keeping the memory alive.

To Zelig Struch, Henry Herschkowitz, Shaul Ladany, Gad Tsabari and Tuvia Sokolsky, and Yehuda Weinstein I am forever united in a deep and abiding indebtedness.

I wish to thank, of course, my parents for their gift of life, my brother Yoram for his gift of patience, my wife Adele for her gift of healing love, my children for their gift of devotion, Adele's cousin Neville for his gift of golf, and Adele's cousin Lynda for her gift of faith. A very special thanks is reserved for my faithful dog Frizo, who keeps me ever in good shape.

Munich Olympic Village

31 Connollystrasse, from the back

Introduction

If you go to the Olympic Village in Munich today, you might not even realize that you have stumbled into a killing field. The village is a lively residential area occupied by immigrants and students and retains that kind of '60's era post-Brutalism, where horizontal lines and symmetry soften the violence of the hard, plain concrete. At first sight, there is no evidence of the terrible event that occurred here just forty years ago.

I visited the village with my elder son Meir in the summer of 2011. Meir only knew about Munich from his classroom history, which meant he knew very little, and he had almost no idea at all of what I went through there.

When we got to 31 Connolly Street, the apartment house where we Israeli athletes were billeted, where our comrades were slain, Meir and I found a plaque that had been placed at the front door, a very plain, straightforward marker, with the events of September 1972 and the names of the slain athletes inscribed in German and in Hebrew. I stood staring at this commemoration for a moment, and then I broke down and began to weep, to sob inconsolably like a baby. Poor Meir. Overcome by the experience, moved beyond words, he was befuddled, but then he had the presence of mind to call my wife, and she talked me out of my stupor.

Afterward, Meir wrote this about his experience:

> *"It was early in the morning when me and my father entered the Olympic village, just a regular day with people hurrying to get to work and other destination; some had come to the village to work in the shops and Konditoreis where 40 years earlier stood the sportsmen's dining room and the cafes and stores where the athletes congregated. It was a normal day. People were going about their lives, with no idea who we were or what this place means to us.*
>
> *I found it hard to believe that this was the place where all the events I had read about and was told about took*

place. My Father called my Mom and told her that we were standing together at the building on Connolly Street in the Olympic Village, where his comrades and he slept and laughed together, and I felt sadness to see my father shiver and to hear his voice tremble as he spoke of the tragedy that he suffered with them.

Then I guess all the feelings he has about this place bubbled up from inside him. I wasn't even born yet at the time of those terrible events, but I could tell that they were worse than he had ever been able to tell us. I had never before seen my father express his feelings regarding this tragedy so deeply as those few moments we were standing there at that building.

We stayed for a little longer before we moved to the other sites, and my father explained to me about all the facilities, and he showed me the Olympic stadium. Seeing all the village facilities, which were built for such a special event whose purpose was sport and friendship, made me wonder how could this lovely purpose be marked with hatred and intolerance?"

This book is for Meir...also for Pazit and for Arik and for my future grandchildren. It is, in fact, for all the children of Israel. We endure great tragedy, yes. But I am proof that so long as we remember, we go on.

CHAPTER 1

Memory

Never shall I forget those moments, which murdered my God and my soul and turned my dreams to dust.

*Elie Wiesel, **Night***

Yosi Romano lifting Zelig Struch

The Israeli team at the Olympic stadium

Memory records personal truths. I look back at the event forty years ago that has defined my life ever since, and I remember, with absolute clarity, conversations, scenes, observations. Then I sit with others who were there, and they have memories that do not resonate for me. Each of us lived through that cataclysmic day and the debilitating aftermath in our own skin. Each of us brought to the day a fated future and walked away from it with a unique history.

I have heard and read reports from the scene at the funeral for five of our fallen comrades, and even though I marched alongside the coffins as they were carried from the transport to the place in Kiryat Shaul Cemetery where they would be interred, even though I was standing with the rest, I did not hear what anyone else heard. My mind was brimming with my own images, with thoughts of Andrei Spitzer, my coach and friend, with the sight of Moshe Weinberg's body as it fell past my window. Everything I heard was tainted by what was in my mind at the time.

Universally, we all have lingering regrets, a sense that we should have known more, should have been better prepared. And we share a sense of betrayal, a feeling of having been somehow thrown to the lions in an arena that should have been safe even for sheep.

Many of us had had feelings of foreboding before the Olympics, before the massacre. I heard somewhere that the most famous was Ilana Romano's. According to someone who claimed to have been there, Ilana and her husband Yossef (Yossi), a powerful weightlifter, threw a party just before the team left Israel for Germany, and at that party, she told him she was terrified for him. My source said that she said that she was sure that something terrible was about to happen to him, especially considering that he had been injured just days before and had to walk on crutches. "You're crazy," he is said to have told her affectionately. "The Germans will have it so well organized, nothing can possibly go wrong."

I can only imagine that when Ilana got the call on the morning of September 5, 1972, and was told the athletes had been taken hostage, she was doubly alarmed. Libyan born Yossi was never one to lie low and wait; she knew that he would have put himself in the line of fire rather than to allow himself to be easily captured, and she was right. Romano was the second of our teammates to die, and he died attempting to save Moshe Weinberg.

But most of our forebodings were less dramatic. In fact, at first, I would have argued strenuously that we had nothing to fear in Munich.

I had studied near Cologne/Köln, Germany years before and had experienced such a warm welcome, I was sure Germany was the perfect place for an Olympic Games. When I was there, I fenced, and I was with colleagues and students who were remarkably pro-Israel, proud to have an Israeli among them.

I had been sent to work at a printing and textile company in a town called Minden, where I hardly expected to find Israelis, fencers or Jews. But I was pleasantly surprised – when I visited the sports shop, I discovered that Minden was home to one of the largest fencing clubs in the area, and I was welcomed for my skills. I met fencers whose parents had been Nazis, and the fencers were warm, though their parents couldn't look me in the eye.

At some point, I injured my back. One of the fencers took me home to the house where he lived on the first floor with his parents, who lived on the second. His parents ignored me, but they didn't bother me.

During the time I was in Minden, I was called home to participate in the 6-Day War. I promised to come back, and when I heard from my friends after the war was over, I learned that during the war, the German fencers in had put up a huge map of the Middle East, and they placed flags on the map, which they moved about as they received the news of our actions. I don't know how they were able to do that, but they were very excited for us. Israel was popular before, but after the war, we earned their abject admiration, having achieved a victory they could hardly imagine for themselves. When I returned twenty years later with my wife Adele – and this was after the Munich Olympics, of course -- my German friends all turned out at the train station to greet me, and the next morning, they returned with food and drink to throw a huge party for my departure.

When I arrived for the Olympics, I felt a kind of homecoming, very safe and secure in the belief that Germans would protect Jews on their soil. I had learned to pity the Germans in a way, to regret they had had to endure Hitler and that the Holocaust happened to them as much as it had happened to us. So, when I arrived for the Games and began to see the flaws in the Olympic Village, I tried not to make too much of it, tried not to let the nagging discomfort overtake my joy.

Looking back, however, I realize how appalled I was at the laxity of security we found in the Olympic Village when we fencers arrived two weeks early for a practice session with the German National team. I could not believe how our assigned house, 31 Connolly Street, was entirely without safety. "Don't worry," everyone told me. "The Germans want to prove they have changed since the war; they won't allow anything to happen to you." So I kept my mouth shut.

I learned later that Shmuel Lalkin, our Head of Delegation, had not kept his mouth shut. He had inspected the premises months before the Olympics and had pronounced the house inappropriate for our lodgings. Further, he requested that there be an armed guard placed at our door, or, at very least, that he be allowed to keep a pistol in his room in Apartment 5. His requests were denied, and though he protested several times, his requests fell on deaf ears.

After it was over, after our comrades were buried in Kiryat Shaul and other cemeteries around Israel, after David Berger's body returned to his parents' home in Cleveland, the stunned numbness faded, and I began to feel anger. For years I was hounded by a rage I couldn't describe, couldn't understand. It changed me, led me to leave fencing and, even after I reemerged in the sport only to quit again, it left me unable to feel that anything – even the birth of my three children – was ever large enough to overshadow or to obliterate the stain of the Munich Massacre.

I was angry at the International Olympic Committee (IOC), angry at IOC President Avery Brundage, angry at the German police and the German Olympic Committee. Most of all, of course, I was angry at the Palestinian terrorists, but I could not forgive my own homeland. The country my father had sacrificed his fencing career to build, the country to which I had given my unabashed allegiance all my life, had let me down.

How could this country, whose very existence was predicated by the Nazi Holocaust, have failed so miserably to protect us? After the Yom Kippur War of 1973, after the dramatic rescue of Israeli citizens from the tarmac in Entebbe, after the Mossad's reprisal against Black September for what happened to us, I became sure that it was no accident that we were sacrificed so. For a long time, I erroneously believed that our government, with so much strength and intelligence, must have deliberately allowed us to be destroyed in Munich at an athletic event that was supposed to be entirely void of politics. We must have been sacrificial lambs for some political purpose, and I was convinced that there was some terrible, clandestine conspiracy.

I was wrong. All the experts now agree that the massacre resulted from a terrible oversight that represented an incredible lapse of competency on the part of the Germans and also on the part of the Israeli government and the Mossad. But we know now that it was as much a surprise and a shock to them as it was to us. The fact that eleven athletes were murdered in Munich and that seven more athletes nearly died with them and were left to dig out from under the shock and savagery of it all were attributable to German stupidity and bad planning, to Israeli overconfidence and paucity of circumspection. But none of it resulted from any malicious or deliberate transgression against us by those we trusted.

That was not so clear to me four years ago when I set out to write this book. I was still furious, still sure that someone owed us some justice. Now I am calmer. I accept that it was a preventable bloodbath, perpetrated by a people who wanted then as they want today to eradicate the State of Israel and who have taken a blood oath to eliminate us from the planet. There were then, as there are now, forces in the world with the power to protect us. They didn't.

Our story is a cautionary tale. So much more, so much worse can come of the kind of complacency that cost my friends their lives, cost their families their sleep, and cost me my happiness. We are still vulnerable, and the world has begun to believe that we Israelis are ourselves terrorists.

While it is politically incorrect to say so these days, we are not terrorists. We are, as we have ever been, survivors. As a people, as a country, and as a culture, Jews have always been the targets of hatred, the demonized scapegoats of others. It has become today, in a way that it has not been for the past fifty years at least, commonplace and acceptable to talk about Jews in very deprecating ways. Bernie Madoff made it popular once again to believe in the shyster-Jew stereotype that has been defining us since Shylock uttered his opening line in *Merchant of Venice* in 1597. "Three thousand ducats," said the moneylender of the Rialto, and thereafter, we Jews were blamed for all the world's financial insecurities.

As a result, the world is blind to the fact that most of the trouble in the Middle East is predicated on irrational, absolute desire on behalf of the Arab world for the end of Israel, for the destruction of the Jews. And the world tends toward complicity in that endeavor.

Which is entirely relevant to my story.

My experience in Munich certainly has portent for the coming storm against the Jews, but in a broader sense, it carries momentous weight in how we tell the story on the fortieth anniversary, how we protect our athletes in London, how we prepare for the rest of the twenty-first Century.

We must never trust a sleeping bear or a quiet tiger. We must be equipped with the best kinds of safeguards known to mankind, and we must be ever ready to do battle even while we make every attempt to avert one.

Most of all, we must learn, as I did, forgiveness. In order to see others realistically, to recognize that they are all potentially both friend and foe, we must learn to see each other as we truly are to one another, to eschew euphemisms, to skirt around whitewashing, to avoid so-called political correctness that seeks to make everything palatable but obscures critical truths.

We must learn tolerance for one another, but at the same time, we must be ever wary and learn intolerance for terror. If we can eliminate terror, we can foster the kind of true understanding and forbearance that will preserve us all.

CHAPTER 2

Time Stands Still in Heaven and in Hell

"Thirty-six years may have separated Germany's two twentieth – century Summer Olympiads, but the 1972 Munich games were conducted very much in the shadow of the 1936 Berlin Olympics. The Munich organizers were determined that everything about their games should be different from those of 1936, reflecting their conviction that an 'entirely new Germany' was hosting the festival."

David Clay Large, **Nazi Games**

Twice in my life the earth's spin came to a halt – once on Opening Day of the 1972 Summer Olympics in Munich and again on the day now known as the Munich Massacre. Though they were separated by days of somewhat normal movement, I remember them as a single event. Each has its own place in the pantheon of my mind, but, hard as I try, I cannot enjoy the first without dreading the second. I cannot revel in the joy of the one without shrinking in terror from the other.

Outside 31 Connollystrasse, day after the massacre

Simcha/Celebration

"One of the bitterest ironies of the tragedy of September 5 is that it derived in part from the Munich organizers' well meaning effort to distinguish their games from those of the Berlin games of 1936. Whereas the 1936 Olympic Village was situated on a heavily guarded army base a good distance from Central Berlin, the Munich Village lay right next to the Olympic Stadium and well within the city limits. It was encircled by a six-foot-high security fence whose gates were locked at midnight but not guarded around the clock. By day entry to the village was almost as easy for autograph hunters as it was for athletes and officials. After midnight athletes who had gone out carousing in town could reenter the village by simply climbing over the fence."

> *David Clay Large,* **Nazi Games**

Saturday, the 26th of August, 1972

"Wake up, fencers!"

My coach, Andrei Spitzer stands below the balcony window of the room I share with my teammate Yehuda Weinstein, yelling as though we are the only people in the place.

Andrei's shouting is jubilant. "Finally...Opening Ceremonies!"

His words make me shiver. The day I have been awaiting most of my life has arrived, and I cannot believe that the day is real, that I am real. I know that we are ready, and I am breathless with anticipation.

Andrei, Yehuda and I arrive at the stadium and stand with our countrymen. As the first Israelis ever to enter a German Olympic stadium, we feel especially triumphant.

Andrei Spitzer is a man with a mission, determined that we should, at every moment, be aware of our diplomatic responsibilities here. "Look at this," he says excitedly. "We go in alphabetical order. That means we get to lead the Iranians into the stadium! I want to hold their hands so the world will see that we are brothers."

The late summer sun prickles my anticipation, and I nearly swoon.

"Listen to that applause," I croak. "It's so loud. If I weren't so elated, I'd be terrified!"

Echoes of drums and cymbals punctuate the marching feet of Bavarian soldiers in ancient costumes, and the tinny blasts of antique pistols rattle their salute; the roar of millions of fans' delight surges every time a team is announced and enters the stadium.

"Only you would chose the word 'terrifying' on a day like today," chuckles Yehuda. "Just follow Henry, and do what Schmuel told us to do at the rehearsal meeting."
As instructed by Schmuel Lalkin, our Head of Delegation, we follow Henry Herschkowitz, our veteran marksman, into the stadium. The warm, humid air stands still, and I am not sure I can breathe.

In an attempt to diffuse my stage fright, I allow to my companions, "Henry's so lucky. I understand why he gets to be the leader – after all, this is his fourth Olympics. But I am a little bit jealous, no matter how much he deserves the honor."

"Just be glad it's him not you carrying the Israeli flag, Pischer," Andrei snickers. He looks especially striking in the Israeli uniform that matches our flag: white shirt, beige pants, blue jacket and silver tie with Olympic rings. "It would hide that punim from all the adoring women out there cheering for you."
I am sharply aware of the small photo of my father inside the left pocket of my jacket, behind the small, hand-sewn Israeli flag, and I place my right hand over it now. My teammates and I raise our white straw hats with their blue-stripe bands, and the multitude salutes us.

The crowd jumps to its feet, cheering, shouting, clapping hands with great excitement to see us marching onto this world stage.

"Listen," I marvel to no one in particular. "I think they are singing Hatikveh along with the big German orchestra!" I am suddenly struck by the portent truth of what I have just said.

Esther Shahamurov, our great sprinter, marches in right behind Henry, flanked by Track and Field coach Amitzur Shapira, and I am not far behind. Our swimmer Shlomit Nir is close by. I look around me and see my fencing teammates Yehuda Weinstein and Andrei Spitzer. We are fanned out, in a kind of orderly arrow formation – like flying geese following their invisible compass – that belies the chaos of emotion in my head.

Sunshine shimmers all around me, washing every image in a kind of glimmering joy. Our wrestlers David Berger, Eliezer Halfin, Mark Slavin and Gad Tsabari with their coach Moshe (Manny/Monye) Weinberg, and referee Yossef Gutfreund glow as they walk and wave. Now I see the weightlifters Yossi Romano and Zeev Friedman with their coach Tuvia Sokolovsky and referee Jacov Springer. My housemates speed walker Dr. Shaul Ladany and marksman Zelig Struch are nearby as is our shooting coach Kehat Shorr. Yitzhak Caspi, deputy leader of our delegation walks beside our team chairman Yitzhak Fuchs, who is flanked by Shmuel Lalkin and Kurt Weil, our team doctor. And in all this exultation of color and light, I cannot stop thinking about how tight my shoes feel.

I am wearing a pair of the most exquisite Italian shoes, hand-crafted of silky-soft leather, and I want to kick them off. I want my feet to be free, to make contact with the earth so I can believe this is real. I want to dig my soles into the new-mown grass and feel the dewy softness between my toes. Then I will know that I am not dreaming.

Andrei shouts over the tumult, "I wish Ankie could be here to see this. It is unbelievable!"

Andrei's young wife and their newborn daughter are with her brother in her hometown in The Netherlands. I nod and wave at no one in particular, seeing, as though through a gauzy veil, thousands of people, faceless, shapeless throngs, who stand or sit in a cacophony of color, bathed in a surreal light emanating from somewhere on the other side of the stadium. A single thundering murmur resounds as myriad voices scream in unison, and party horns enthusiastically cheer the athletes on, welcoming even us Jews into this Olympic stadium. We are among friends.

I close my eyes and imagine the joy flickering in my father's eyes, mesmerized by the image of this moment playing on Israeli television. I touch my jacket pocket again. This embrace belongs to him too; this Israeli flag flying over the Olympic Stadium is his achievement as well as mine. The orchestra plays Hava Nagila, and everyone in our delegation joins hands. I am full to bursting. The air is hot, but I am cool. Everything in the world is exactly as it should be at this moment. I am marching into this stadium in Germany thirty years after Hitler tried to annihilate my people. I can feel great electricity, a connectedness to every life in this stadium. We proud first Olympians from the young country of Israel are proof to the world that we Jews have survived our Holocaust, and we are stronger than ever; we are here as Israeli Jewish athletes, ready to compete against the best athletes in the world. I am dizzy in the swirl of it, and I want this moment never to end.

I look over at Andrei, and I see he is weeping with joy. "You know what, Dani? When I get to Heaven, this is exactly what I will find."

As though his words have cued the sky, a strange darkness gathers. Yehuda and I look upward and are awestruck by a multitude of flapping wings swooshing out of cages into the thick, inert air now churning with life. Hundreds of white doves leave the stadium, to inform the world that the XXth Olympiad has begun!

For a split second all is quiet, then a round of gunfire – another salute – and then the explosion of the crowd, a single giant, roaring entity, standing, screaming, shouting, stamping, beating the bleachers, blaring whistles and kazoos, heralding trumpets, before the mass exodus from the stadium begins, and hordes of humans pour forth into the Olympic Village.

****

Then, in my mind, there is a long, terrible silence before another explosion, another round of gunfire, and this time there is no celebration, only a deathwatch.

Shoah/Disaster

"The German failure has no modern equivalent. The amateurishness, negligence, miscalculations, and mistakes made in the management of the crisis are unparalleled. To this day, no one has ever claimed responsibility for the failure to stop the Olympic massacre: not the Bavarian government, not the Federal Republic of German, nor any other German office."

Aaron Klein, **Striking Back**

Tuesday, the 5th of September, 1972

The sun has risen and set, and a lifetime has transpired. It is already Tuesday, and I am enveloped in pre-dawn darkness, suddenly awake. Something has exploded outside. People are shouting.

I can't see anything through the window, but I'm shaking uncontrollably. The blast ripped me from deep sleep, made deeper by the exhaustion of a day of training and a night of too much drinking. I can't remember falling asleep, but now I can't get myself to come out of my fog, and I can't stop shaking.

"What was that, Dani?"

"I can't see anything, Yehuda. Maybe the South Americans upstairs are celebrating."

"If you really believe that, why are you trembling?"

A deadly silence descends. We cannot breathe, waiting to hear something more. Nothing.

"Look Yehuda, whatever it was, it's quiet now. Let's try to go back to sleep."

Twenty minutes later, having barely fallen into a fitful sleep, I am awakened again. Before I am fully conscious, Yehuda is already standing next to my bed.

A sound like no other strafes at my insides.

"This time I recognize that noise," Yehuda is shouting over the din.

He's right. This is a sound you can't mistake once you've heard it.

"Machine gun fire."

"Jesus, Dani. Someone is firing machine guns in our building."

"I know. The walls are quaking."

The building sways. I run around my room in my underwear, trying to see out the window. Our door flies open. Henry Herschkowitz, who is staying in the room next to ours, runs in.

"I heard a gun cocking, right outside my window," exclaims Herschkowitz. "It woke me up. I can see what it is now, and we're in deep shit here, you guys. This is bad. Something terrible is happening, and it's happening to us."

"Over here," Yehuda murmurs.

We go join him at the window. The dawn has cast a watery pallor on the ground below us. Images are emerging from the darkness.

Herschkowitz can't stop pacing. "See that guy down there with the wide, broad hat? He's carrying a machine gun, holding a hand grenade!"

THUD.

Something with enormous weight seems to have hit the pavement outside.

"Shit." Herschkowitz, squinting into the dissolving darkness, grabs his head as though he's having a stroke. "That looks like Moshe. Lying on the ground. I think that's Monye."

I look where he is pointing. It takes a moment for my eyes to capture the scene, but it is soon apparent that oh dear God, he's right. Moshe Weinberg, the Wrestling Coach, is sprawled at the gunman's feet. A fountain of blood pours forth from Weinberg's body, and it pools in the cracks and dips in the pavement, flows onward over the concrete riverbanks nearby.

I push the window open a bit to see if I can learn anything at all. Nothing. I pull the window back and crawl into the room on my hands and knees. Electric light emanates from Apartment 3; it seeps out around the edges of the doors and windows. If I bang on the wall, perhaps I can warn them.

"What's going on, Dani? Is it too late? No one's responding." Herschkowitz has sat down and is riveted to the floor.

"I can't tell. But we better be quiet. What if they don't know we're in here?"

The balcony door is slightly ajar. I crawl over and press against it while I cock my ear, leaning as far out as I can. There are German policemen talking right outside.

"Sie sind Kommandotruppen des Schwarzen Septembers..."

Black September. I know that name.

"Palestinians, Dani," says Yehuda coolly. "They're Palestinian terrorists."

"What are they doing here? This is the Olympics for God's sake."

This can't be happening, I think to myself. We're in Germany. The Germans want to prove to us that Jews are safe in their land. Surely this can only backfire on these masked villains.

I go back to my bedroom and dress in our team's uniform warm-up suit.

Yehuda follows me. "What the hell are you doing?

"Changing. If I am going to die, I want to be found in the colors of Israel."

Die. If I am going to die. My father's face appears in front of me. I can't die. That would kill him.

I stop breathing so I can hear anything they might be saying outside. I dare not even whisper to the others. So far we are safe, or at least we are unmolested here in our apartment, Apartment #2. I wonder where the closest payphone is. I suddenly want to call home, to hear my parents' voices.

Instead I hear policemen's voices, discussing the situation, drifting into our room.

"Ja. Schwarzer September...um den Angriff Palästinensischer Terroristen...

...auf die israelische Mannschaft..."

I only hear fragments, but I begin to piece it together.

The Black September organization, a faction of Palestinian terrorists, has deliberately attacked the Israeli delegation. Two Israelis are already dead. Damn! Moshe and who else? A team of German police has been called in to talk to the hostages and then to contact the Israeli government. One of the policemen sounds very frightened, saying that the gunmen have vowed to kill every Israeli man in Connollystrasse 31 if two hundred Palestinian prisoners now being held in Israel are not set free by 9 a.m.

My athletic training has taught me how important it is to keep my head, to stay calm. My military training has taught me that no situation is hopeless till it's over.

"We need to think, Yehuda. What're we gonna do? We can't just run. We have to find a way into their apartment. We've got to help the others."

"No, Dani. We can't. All we can do is find a way out."

I am struck by how cool and collected he is, so unperturbed. Though he's much younger than I am, he shows no signs of stress or vexation, almost as though he's fearlessly taking the matter in his stride.

I cannot imagine that my government will give in to any terrorists' demands. It is undoubtedly up to us to save ourselves. Shouldn't we also save our teammates? I must remain focused.

I concentrate on my breathing. Slow, deep breaths. I will not lose control.

All but one of us from Apartment #2 are together now. We still hear nothing and see nothing in #3, so we have no idea what is happening with the wrestlers there, but we know we must try to get out of here. Yehuda, Henry Herschkowitz, Zelig Shtruch and I head for the other side; we mean to get to the balcony. We don't want to use the stairs, sure that the creakiness might surely arouse the terrorists' attention.

We creep along, staying close to the floor, desperate to keep any of the expanding morning light from illuminating our movements to the outside world. As we get close to the balcony once again, I see, standing right above my head, another gunman holding a machine gun just a couple feet away.

They will surely discover us here. How can they have overlooked us till now? How many of them can there be? Are we surrounded? Is there even a hope for escape should we decide to grab it?

I slide, commando style, away from the balcony to the other side of the room. I look at Henry, our Opening Day flag bearer. Poor Henry. He is a sweet, gentle man, a Romanian watchmaker, who lives in a placid world of ticking timepieces. He is white as the wall, muttering to himself, obviously nearly paralyzed with fear. "What are you trying to say, Henry?" I sign to him. He points to the two rifles, Zelig's and his weapons, standing against the doorjamb.

He uses some very small arm movements and whispers a few words. What he is suggesting is that one of the marksmen take a shot at the gunmen to distract them so that the rest of the prisoners they have taken, our friends and teammates, can spring out and escape. We consider this for a moment. We are losing time.

"No," I hiss. "Too risky." We don't know what condition they're all in. They could easily be too slow to get away. Then we will have accomplished nothing but drawing attention to all of us. We'll be found, and that might induce the terrorists to call in more gunmen to wreak havoc on the hostages they have already taken.

"I can't leave them, Yehuda." The words I am saying are so faint, I can't even hear them; Yehuda must be reading my lips. "There has to be something we can do to free them. If we turn our backs, we betray them. We are righteous men. How can we leave them in the jaws of the beast?

"We have to run," says Yehuda. In his cool, collected way, he identifies the crux of our dilemma. "Dani, you don't have any power. You don't have anything to offer. If you try anything, at the very least, you will die, and then what will you have gained? We must run. The way out is clear – we'll head out through the garden. There are policemen out there. They can help us."

"But who can help them?" I point toward our teammates' apartments.

"We must save ourselves, Dani. It's all we can do."

"They've got Andrei, Yehuda. They've got our Andrei."

"We can only do what we can do, Dani."

It is an immutable truth. If we stay or if we attempt some heroics, we will all die. Our collective Olympic dreams will be extinguished in a single firestorm, all our future children denied conception, leaving all our parents with nothing but the knowledge that their sons were slaughtered in one fell swoop. My comrades' fate is out of our hands, but my own destiny, for the moment, still belongs to me.

God help us all.

"Dani," Herschkowitz tries to speak softly, but I fear he is too loud. "Ladany's still asleep in his room. We've gotta wake him up."

I almost forgot about Dr. Ladany, our speed walker. This man, the veteran of three Olympics, a professor at Beer Sheva University, sleeps the sleep of the dead, hearing nothing, disturbed by nothing.

No choice any longer. Now that an eerie silence has blanketed our apartment, now that the predawn stillness has muted even the last nightingale, we must go down those squeaky stairs. Besides the fact that Dr. Ladany is sleeping on the first floor, the only escape is through his room to the garden and out.

"Not yet. Not yet! Please not yet." It's Zelig Shtruch. He's in a panic.

"I have to brush my teeth," he pleads. "I can't move until I've brushed my teeth. I can't. I can't."

We wait for him before we begin to descend the stairs.

As anticipated, the wooden steps are terribly noisy. "Let's all go barefoot," Yehuda mouths wordlessly. "It's our only hope."

A short flight of stairs, but it takes us an eternity to descend. While I am tiptoeing down the steps, I look outside again, and I see Moshe Weinberg still on the ground. Paramedics are there around him now, and their behavior toward him confirms the policemen's reports that he is dead. Blood has flooded the pavement – poor Weinberg seems to have been shot in the face and in the chest with a machine gun, though it's hard to make out the details. I strain to see more of him, but the policemen obscure him from me. He cannot be a pretty sight, but I feel I need to look at him, to remember. The paramedics are lifting him onto a stretcher; perhaps he's not dead. Yehuda grabs my arm and pulls me along.

We go together to Dr. Ladany's room.

"Dr. Ladany," Zelig whispers in his ear. "Wake up." No response.

Herschkowitz shakes his shoulder. "Shaul, wake up. We've gotta get out of here." Still the doctor does not move.

Zelig Shtruch shakes him too, and Yehuda finally signals me that we will have to lift him up. We raise him to a standing position and persist until his body realizes what is going on, and he begins to awaken.

"What?" He shouts. "What's going on?" Zelig puts his hand over the doctor's mouth.

"Sssh, Doctor, you must be quiet. We are in trouble..."

"Leave me alone. What do you want? What...??

The doctor regains his wits after a few moments, and, though he struggles with us a bit, we manage to get him up and into enough clothing to make him decent.

After what seems like a very long time, he is finally ready, and we edge out slowly, one at a time, toward the garden and into the darkness.

"Let the older guys go first, Dani. We'll help them."

"Good idea, Yehuda. Then you go. I'll come last."

Yehuda is just emerging from our apartment when a scuffle of feet startles him. He flattens his body against the concrete, blends into its colorlessness, and buries his face in its coarseness. I hold my breath. If they see him...

We wait. How long? A lifetime. I watch Yehuda, whose expressionless body seems willing to wait forever.

I see a policeman motion to Yehuda, and my heart stops. Yehuda stays stock still, and the policeman looks up at the rooftop where the gunmen are and finally seems to understand the situation. Now he turns his attention to the other escapees, who are slowly coming into view.

Nothing happens; the gunmen take no notice. Yehuda slides soundlessly outside to safety. The policeman sees him and motions for him to come forward. Yehuda breaks into a silent run-walk and joins our comrades. The wary, helpless police receive them all warmly, and escort them to safety in another building.

Now it is my turn. I creep outside, and I am just about to break into a run; I can feel my feet touching the cool, comforting cleanliness of the grass, and I fight an urge to simply roll around in it, to wrap myself in its dewy sweetness and feel safe, when I look up to see a guy holding a rifle, looking directly into my eye.

I am sure he will shoot me. We hold each other in one another's gaze for what feels like a very long time. I feel him enter my body, and I enter his. I understand what he wants of me; he is a trained killer, poised for the slaughter. But neither of us can move.

The gunman and I are paralyzed, suspended in this moment, but the world continues as if we two do not exist. The sun persists in rising in the sky, traffic under the complex increases, lights come on in the apartments around us, garbage collectors and maintenance workers clatter about the grounds, and runners take their morning exercise along the pathways; from someplace, I smell coffee and olives, and I feel as though I will surely faint.

****

But I didn't faint. I ran.

When I got to the ground, in the corner of my eye, I caught a policeman motioning to me surreptitiously, still careful not to draw attention to our flight.

I joined my housemates at the guard station, and the police took us first to the main office of the Olympic Village and then to a special interrogation room where we described for them exactly what we had seen and heard.

Our teammates were in terrible peril. We knew that, and it made us both grateful and uneasy. We few – two fencers, two riflemen and a speed walker – were safe. Each of us understood that we had seen with our own eyes what the world was at that moment trying to imagine, but we were impatient with the questioning. Madmen with machine guns were holding our comrades, including my dear friend Andrei Spitzer. All we wanted was to get back to the compound where we could stand our vigil.

****

The sun has not yet risen as we return to the Israeli apartment building at Connollystrasse 31. The sequestered little world of the Olympic Village is just awakening from the bliss of their sleep-blessed ignorance. We walk numbly, only vaguely aware that the grounds are deserted. No athletes scurry to morning workouts, and no officials rush to their morning meetings. All competitions, all Olympic activities are momentarily suspended, but, of course, we don't really care about that.

I feel my father's fear in my stomach, and though I am in a hurry to get back to where my friends are being held, I look for a telephone. I know I must get word to my family right away because the strain of thinking I might be dead will be too much for my poor father. Worse, I am afraid he will hear misinformation on the television, and I want him to know I am okay. The fastest way I can think of to make contact is to call a friend of mine here in Munich and ask him to get word to Israel. Calling my friend calms me a little for a moment; at least I can stop worrying about my father, but it feels so unreal to be speaking to someone outside the catastrophe.

From my friend I learn a few more details: the Palestinian spokesperson Issa has confirmed that two Israelis are dead and that he plans to kill the rest of his hostages if his demands are not met. But he has not said how many Israelis are in his custody, and he will not name the dead.

Of course, I know one was the gentle giant Moshe Weinberg, but who else? I ask my friend to promise my parents I'll call as soon again as I can, and I head back to Connollystrasse.

Esther Shahamurov and Shlomit Nir rush over to me. We embrace, weeping.

"Dani, over in the women's compound, we didn't hear a thing. We came as soon as we –" Esther sobs, unable to say anymore.

I am suddenly enveloped in a manly hug, and I gasp as I realize it is wrestler Gad Tsabari. He and weightlifter Tuvia Sokolovsky, both initially imprisoned with the others, have managed to escape.

Gad speaks to me as though through a thundering waterfall. His words are drowning me. "They had us like sheep, you know? But Moshe and Romano jumped them – Yossi was actually beating at them with his crutch – and I thought I would rather die running than be trapped. So I ran. Someone was shouting at me in Hebrew and Arabic, and there were bullets raining down on me, but I kept running, through the parking lot. Then, suddenly, I saw that I was safe."

I nod, holding him in my arms even more tightly than before, and I am a bit embarrassed by his weeping. After a moment I turn my attention to our weightlifting coach Tuvia Sokolsky.

"Tuvia," I stammer. "How did you get away?"

"Gutfreund heard them breaking down the door. He made himself a barrier and gave me time to smash a window. I jumped out."

I am having some difficulty grasping the details. "I heard the police say two of our guys were dead. I saw Moshe..."

"Romano," Tsabari groans.

"Yossi?" I gasp incredulously. "But he can't be dead. He's only 31, and his children..."

We stand there, not knowing what else to say, hardly daring to whisper any more to one another. The Germans enforce a 50-foot distance between the compound and us, and we await a miracle.

It feels like we've been here for days already, but it's only 9 a.m. The police call our contingent together – now Schmuel Lalkin and some of the other officials from the IOC join us. They report that the Germans have been successful in negotiating with the terrorists. What we hadn't known beforehand was that the fedeyeen had threatened to kill the hostages at 9 if by then they had not received news of the liberation of all Palestinians held in Israeli prisons. Now we have till Noon.

They also definitively identify the Palestinian gunmen. They are Black September, a fairly new faction of the Palestinian Liberation Organization, a group we don't know a lot about except that their name commemorates an action that King Hussein of Jordan took against Palestinians in his country; they are determined to claim a homeland at all costs. At this moment I care very little about who they were. All I can think about is what they are likely to do to our comrades.

One of the German officials – is he the Chief of the German police? - says that the Germans' objective is to buy time.

"We are sure that we'll convince your government to make the necessary concessions in order to free your teammates. Perhaps these Black Septembrists will just get tired and hungry and go home.

Yehuda nudges me to silence because I mutter something out loud. I mean no disrespect, but I have served in the Israeli air force, I was on active duty in the 1967 War. Even if I hadn't, I would know what reassures every Israeli citizen: Golda Meir will never consider negotiating with terrorists. We would not want her to. Israel's existence is far too fragile to allow her enemies to manipulate events so easily.

And we also know that terrorists don't get tired and hungry, filled as they are with the will of Allah. So I find no relief from the fear that eats at my belly.

Waiting. Waiting. Forever waiting. Standing, sitting on the ground, mesmerized by the sheer force of the waiting. We hardly speak to one another. Someone – I don't think it is one of us – brings water, food; none of us has an appetite for anything but information.

We stop breathing every time the Palestinian called Issa emerges from hiding to speak with negotiators. He carries a machine gun in one hand and a grenade, its pin out, in the other; on his head is a balaclava, like a ski mask, which covers his features. I can't get over how small, how puny he seems. I think I could overtake him if only we could figure out a way to disarm him.

No time passes, but it is noon. Even though Golda Meir has requested that the games be suspended until the terrorists are defeated, the Germans have determined that no matter what, the Olympics must continue as planned; as though we do not exist in this prison of woe, the games go will on, oblivious to us. Somewhere in an alternate universe that is right here in the same complex, there is cheering and celebrating for a winner of an event, and there is disappointment for the defeated opponent, but those athletes are engaged in the pleasure of their achievements, while we witness the death of all joy.

Issa is on the balcony, demanding food.

I hear the Germans hatching another brilliant plan. This police chief surmises that now they have a good opportunity to get in and see what's going on, count the gunmen, check on the hostages. So the chief of police and a detective dress themselves in the hotel chefs' clothing to deliver an abundance of food. It's actually a kind of comic relief in a way, seeing those awkward "chefs" gingerly carrying boxes of food.

Then if I were not so deeply depressed, I'd be laughing at their naiveté. They think it will take such an effort to get the food inside that the guards will ask for the help of the "chefs" and allow them in. Issa, of course, is not so easily fooled. His own men take the boxes one at a time, and no one from the outside is invited in.

This back and forth negotiating and playing for time will surely never end. Yet we all dread the inevitable black moment when the ultimata will cease. That's when hell will surely explode from within.

My housemates encourage me to eavesdrop on the Germans as they huddle for instructions. They call in more police, dressed as snipers, and send them onto the rooftops to surround the apartment where the hostages are being held. They look and behave like a bad company of Keystone Cops in second-rate silent movie. There they are, dressed in athletes' warm-up suits but carrying huge rifles, placing themselves on the rooftops and balconies. All around us, myriad news crews swarm, filming every move the police are making. There is a monitor nearby, and we can see what the police are doing because their action is being broadcast on every major channel in Europe! The Palestinians are watching too, you can bet on that.

Issa shrieks at the Germans that if the police don't vacate the perimeters, all hostages will be shot immediately. The Germans instantly comply.

Sometime in the middle of this horrible day I lift my heavy, sunbaked eyelids upward to see a door opening onto a balcony outside the apartment-prison. Andrei Spitzer emerges into view. The Germans have asked the gunmen to prove that the hostages are still alive. I want to scream.

Because Andrei speaks good English and perfect German, the officials are questioning him. "Is everyone all right?" His voice is heavy and hoarse. "As well as can be expected. " When they ask him to name the other prisoners, I see a gun butt raised behind him and brought down on his head; he falls and disappears.

The sun has set now, but I have not moved. It's 8:30 p.m.; the negotiators have just struck an agreement with Black September. Something is about to happen.

As I understand it, the plan is that a bus will be brought to the underground entrance of Apartment #1, 31 Connollystrasse, where the hostages are incarcerated. The bus will collect the terrorists and their hostages and take them to the Village's main entrance where a helicopter will meet them and fly them to an airport outside of Munich. From there, a civilian airliner is supposed to take them all to a sympathetic country, possibly to Egypt, where they can wait for further developments. I don't like the sound of it.

But the Germans seem relieved to be moving the crisis away from the Olympic Village. Now the games, which have finally been suspended, will resume. The Germans want the world to see that they have the situation under control, that they are getting things back to normal.

Three helicopters land just thirty yards from where we stand in the compound. The media circus is bizarre. There are journalists with microphones, with cameras, with television crews surrounding us as though we were waiting for film stars to arrive on a red carpet. A large bus pulls up in front of the landing area, and the terrorists appear with our comrades in tow.

I can't hear anything over the roaring copter blades and my beating heart. The hostages -my friends - are shoved forward, their hands tied together, one long rope connecting them to one another. The terrorists pull, push and wrench at their captives. Every few feet, a masked marauder hits one or more of the hostages with a rifle butt. This is for me the most traumatic moment of them all.

I am impotent. My friends, my teammates, my compatriots are being loaded into the first two helicopters. I shout at them in Hebrew, saying nothing, just words. I weep. People gather around me, trying to calm me down, but I am agitated, and nothing can help me. I feel myself standing in a black hole, a huge force pulling at me, sucking me down. My mouth moves, but no sound emerges. I want to scream, to fight, to bite someone's fingers off, but I cannot move.

And in the distant near darkness, the last rays of the sun illuminate my friends, trussed for slaughter, in the seat of those helicopters, now flying away. I know that there can be no good end to this.

As the helicopters leave the ground, I realize that the Germans have missed the one, brief opportunity they might have had for a successful rescue attempt. In the moment that the hostages were being loaded into the helicopters, we were all so close, we might have been even able to reach out and touch their faces. At that moment, if we had shouted in Hebrew for the hostages to run, the Germans would have had a chance to shoot the captors. Perhaps in that way some of our dear ones might have escaped.

Instead, I just wave goodbye.

****

The first two helicopters took off, and then the third. It was too dark for us to see who got on the last helicopter, but we assumed they were Germans. Later we found out that Zvi Zamir, our Director of Mossad was on that helicopter. He had come to Germany to supervise the negotiations, but the Germans were not listening to him. As the copters were taking off, we only knew that we were terrified for our teammates.

The Israelis had offered to send troops to Munich to storm the compound and free the hostages, but the Germans wanted to make it clear that they could handle the crisis on their own, so they refused, and they allowed Zamir in only as an observer and an advisor, and as an advisor, he was ignored.

The helicopters proceeded to Fürstenfeldbrück Air Field, at a military base outside Munich. The whole world, now watching on television, held its collective breath with us, and word came swiftly back that all the hostages were safe. Schmuel Lalkin, the Head of the Israeli Delegation himself, delivered the happy news. The Germans had made a successful rescue attempt, all terrorists were dead, and our comrades were alive and well and already on their way back to the Olympic Village.

We were wildly ecstatic. We danced, we shouted, we sang Hava Nagila! Even though our dear Yossi Romano and Moshe Weinberg were dead, what mattered was that all the others were alive, that in a few hours they would be restored to their families.

All had ended at last, and all was well. We could finally leave our vigil behind, and we went to buy champagne for our celebration. The champagne was delicious, but we sobered very quickly, reflecting on what we had been through and on the enormous loss of Weinberg and Romano.

Our team doctor, a veteran of many terror attacks, brought us relaxants and anti-depressants, but we didn't want to sleep. We were too tightly wound and preferred to stay together in a more public setting, in the reception area of the Olympic Village. Our German friends brought us food and stayed with us, talking softly until we all dozed off just minutes before the bad news found us.

At 3 a.m., we were startled awake by Schmuel Lalkin's return. He wore the expression of someone who has been tortured and left for dead. He told us that the earlier reports were false. In truth, he said, the Germans had bungled the ambush; then he told us the whole story of their ill-laid plans. Lalkin spoke slowly, his words weighing on his tongue, pulling the corners of his mouth almost to his chin.

Unbeknownst to any of us, the Germans had vowed that the terrorists would not leave Germany alive. I learned much later that earlier in the day, Magdi Gohary, the Egyptian advisor to the Arab League, was allowed into the apartment to speak with the terrorists, to check on the condition of the hostages. The German police had requested that Gohary take a count of the terrorists, and he had counted five gunmen.

But when the helicopters appeared in the compound, and the masked gunmen herded the hostages out into the waning daylight, Manfried Schreiber, the Chief of Police, realized with terrible alarm that Gohary's intelligence had been incorrect. There were eight gunmen, and each had a machine gun. But the correction came too late; his instructions had already set a terrible blunder in motion.

At Fürstenfeldbrück Airport, hidden in the airplane provided for the Palestinians, five German sharpshooters waited in ambush. The plan, of course, was that each German policeman would pick off one terrorist quickly enough that the hostages would be safely freed. Unfortunately, the Germans were sorely undermanned and under prepared for the operation. They were not trained snipers, and they had no experience in this kind of combat. They did manage to successfully obliterate the five fedeyeen their intelligence had alerted them to, but the three whom Gohary had not seen responded to the attack by turning their guns on the Israeli athletes.

In the first helicopter, the assassins emptied their weapons into the men still tied down in their seats. Knowing the police would close in quickly, they then threw their grenades into the second helicopter, and it burst into flames, spitting white-hot shrapnel and crisply burned pieces of our comrades out onto the airfield.

I remember thinking Lalkin was far away as he recounted this tale, speaking to us from somewhere under the ground, his throat engorged with gravel. I had the feeling that the world was swallowing itself, and I was falling into a deep crevasse. My ears pounded, and my heart strained in my chest. I could not speak or cry. The truth was far too horrible to be real.

They were all dead. All. Dead.

****

The next day we went back into the stadium. Over 100,000 people crowded the stands this time for a far bleaker ceremony than the opening day's – athletes from the Games, guests, officials, the Chancellor and the President of Germany, military personnel from around the world, ambassadors, dignitaries, celebrities. We were there to remember the slain athletes, to honor their memory, to acknowledge our loss, but I remember feeling no solace.

The music, played not by an oom-pah band but rather by the German Philharmonic Orchestra, was Beethoven's Eroica, the Third Symphony. It sounded far more victorious than I felt, far more heroic than our slain, martyred comrades had been allowed to be. Over my head, a wash of voices, speechmakers droning blah-blah-blah, words I could not focus on. All the dignitaries spoke, and I am sure they said beautiful things about how the Olympics had been compromised, how we were all diminished by the deaths of these brave men, how the world would never truly recover. But I could not listen.

I was too distracted by what I would have to do as soon as the service ended.

Meanwhile, all through the terrible day of September 5 and into the next day, there was discussion regarding the fate of the XXth Olympiad. The Israeli government insisted that the Germans stop the games, but the Olympic Federation had to consider a variety of dissenting opinions.

Like many of the athletes, I believed that the Games should go on. In the first place, we felt it was a critically important message to send to the terrorists. No one should ever surrender to terror; no event should be cancelled to honor terrorists' aims. Life should go on as though the monsters did not exist. If you ignore them, they have less power.

In the second place, and this was of paramount importance to me, the athletes who had traveled from all over the world to compete in the games should not have to surrender their dreams, sacrifice their hard work, relinquish their gains to the Arabs. They should not be expected to give up. They had been working tirelessly for four years at least, were some of the most famous athletes in the world, and if they were asked to forsake their Games, they would only resent Israel. Such a decision would only stoke in some deep corner of their hearts the coals of a hatred that The Olympics works so hard to eradicate. We Israeli athletes were content with the committee's decision to continue the Games.

When Prime Minister Golde Meir called us home, however, our Olympic Games ended. We would be excluded from the final competitions and the closing ceremonies. We would have appreciated the opportunity to carry the Israeli flag, now adorned with a black strip draped across its center, through the stadium in the company of the other flags in the closing ceremonies, but Mrs. Meir wanted us home. And before we returned, we had one last, terrible responsibility to accomplish.

As per our instructions from Mrs. Prime Minister, we went back to the compound at Connollystrasse 31, back to the apartments where our teammates had been captured, to collect all our own things and to prepare the eleven victims' belongings to be presented to their grieving families.

It's an experience that lives in me, as do the Opening Ceremonies, as do the awful siege and vigil, in the present tense.

****

Yehuda and I have arrived in the building, and we look around us, trying to imagine what happened. Did we dream all we thought transpired here? How could we be alive?

The rooms are in chaos. Nothing remains in the closets; everything our friends brought to Munich lies strewn about the floor. Books, clothing, toothbrushes, deodorant, Band-Aids, and shoes zigzag about the room, covered in drying, caking, spatters and puddles of blood. Ants and spiders crawl about decaying abandoned food.

The worst of the madness is in Andrei Spitzer's room, where Yossi Romano bled to death. Poor, dear Yossi. He wasn't even supposed to be here at the Olympics.

I take a deep breath and try to contain my emotions, but I am choking on the smell, and I lose control. Oh, Yossi – Yossef – Romano! The gentle giant, an artist, an interior designer whose sport belied his inner softness, was having a problem with his knee, a meniscus injury. Our doctor treated the injury, gave Romano crutches and ordered him home, but Yossi insisted on staying with the team.

This morning, while we waited, Gad told us that Yossi attacked the terrorists with his crutches so forcefully that he hurt one of the guards, and he even succeeded in disarming one of the terrorists, but they took his crutches away and shot him with a machine gun at very close range. The bullets passed through Yossi's body and lodged themselves in a wall.

I walk back to Yehuda's and my room, and I stumble around in a daze, remembering the darkness, then the explosion, then being awake, feeling that I must navigate through an earthquake. I look at the wall that adjoins Spitzer's bedroom, and there, behind the headboard of what was my bed, is the hole left by the bullet – the forensics team has taken the bullet away, but there is no mistaking the form of the hole – that passed through Yossi's body. I shudder, and as quickly as I can move, I return to Spitzer's room, the scene of the crime.

There I confront the most poignant scene of all. In the midst of the horrific mess of that apartment, fathers' gifts for their young children are splayed forlornly about the floor. Here now is the real harbinger of the deeper pain that awaits us all when we step off our plane back home. Toys, dolls, and games; the flags and caps traded among the international competitors, the books and knick-knacks, the brightly colored scarves and carefully chosen jewelry that would have been presented with love and pride, all tug at my emotions, which I am not even trying to conceal.

I pull my camera from my bag and take a photograph of this mêlée. I want never, ever to forget.

****

Yehuda and I cleaned the room then and packed the scattered personal effects into suitcases, writing names of our fallen brothers on luggage tags in preparation for the flight back to Tel Aviv with the valises and the bodies.

German President Walter Schell came to the airport to see the remnants of the Israeli Olympic team off at Munich's Franz Josef Strauss International Airport. Wearing our uniforms, we stood at attention while German officials loaded ten coffins into the front of the specially chartered El Al aircraft that had come to take us home. We were silent, all of us dreading how we would feel when we met the waiting families and friends, dreading how it would feel to watch as those ten coffins covered by Israeli flags were unloaded from the airplane. There was an eleventh coffin, but it did not travel with us.

Weightlifter David Berger's body had already been sent back to the United States, where he had recently graduated from Columbia Law School; we had said our good byes to him at the gate where his body was loaded onto the plane bound for his parents' hometown near Cleveland, Ohio.

On the relentless flight home, my thoughts were deafening. No one could talk; speech eluded us. For most of us, the sheer effort of being was so great that we could not move our mouths. Most of us had had no sleep since the ordeal began, but anyone who slept at all slept only fitfully and intermittently all the way to Tel Aviv.

When our plane arrived at Ben Gurion Airport, I strained to see out the window, and the sight that I beheld astonished me. We passengers had to be transferred from the plane across the tarmac into the terminal by bus, and looking out that window, I realized that there was no way for us to get to a bus. A massive multitude obscured the tarmac. Thousands of people had come to meet the plane; it felt as if all of Israel was there. I searched the crowd for a glimpse of my parents and brother, wanting desperately to run to them, shouting with exultation that I was alive; but I knew that we must swallow our joy and share in the crushing, savage despair with our countrymen. I burst into tears that would not stop falling.

We stepped down into a bristling, stark, deafening sea of silence. I had expected a great keening, a universal moan, a country weeping in unison. But instead, whether out of respect or out of sheer shock, there was this absolute, white soundlessness.

Then the drone of ten small army trucks drilled into the air, and the vehicles cut through the sea of mourners. A single coffin was loaded onto each truck, and we survivors climbed aboard where we were assigned. Yehuda and I rode into the terminal on the truck carrying Andrei Spitzer, and all my senses were scraped by the whirr of the truck engine, the gravel under the wheels. Like my nation of mourners, I was struck dumb.

That night, in the safety of my parents' home, surrounded by my closest family and friends, I still found it impossible to talk. All night we sat up together, silently remembering, not even whispering among ourselves.

The next day, Erev Rosh Hashanah, was the funeral that obscured celebration of our holiday. Along with the apples and honey meant to sweeten the New Year, the people of Israel were forced to ingest the bitter salt of burying our dead heroes, the innocent athletes gunned down in the prime of their glory. Everyone in Israel realized that we were headed into a sad year.

For me, that New Year's Eve was the beginning of a long and painful night that lasted for nearly thirty-four years.

In all those years, no one asked me what it was like to be there, to have watched impotently as it all went down, to have escaped inexplicably. No one asked, and I would have been unable to answer in any case. I had no words to offer.

Nizkor – Memoriam

*"On the day after the murders, at a memorial service for the
dead Israeli athletes, Avery Brundage, still president of the IOC,
announced that the Munich games would go on as scheduled
after a single day of mourning. By way of justifying this decision,
he (with breathtaking insensitivity) lumped the murder of the
Israelis together with the threat by the black African states to
boycott the Munich Olympics unless Rhodesia were excluded.
Having given in to the 'naked political blackmail' of the Africans,
Brundage said, the IOC could not buckle to Arab terrorism: 'The
Games Must Go On.'"*

> *David Clay Large, **Nazi Games***

At first, though I had no words to express what I had seen, I
could think about nothing else but the Olympics. My memories
flooded my awareness with images of all that we had been
through, but I was continually astounded, appalled, bewildered
by my overwhelming question: why had I survived? I could make
no sense of my miracle.

I was exceedingly aware of where the miracle began,
however, and that bothered me too because I felt the hand of
God, and I found no comfort there.

I returned in my mind to the day we arrived in Munich for
the first time, the day we chose our apartment.

Over the years I had been competing in Germany off and on
since the days when I was a journeyman printer in Menden, a
town whose proficient fencing team had welcomed me as a
member and who later invited me back for tournaments, which
greatly enhanced my quest to become an Olympic athlete. In the
months immediately preceding the Olympic games, I had
attended several high level European championships and had
beaten many of the top-ranked German fencers. I had even
defeated Friedrich Wessel, the World Champion Foil fencer.

For that reason, when Yehuda Weinstein and I were selected
to represent Israel at the Games and Andrei Spitzer was

appointed as our coach, the Germans invited us to Munich two weeks before the start of the Games. We would reside in the Olympic Village and train with the Germans, then fly back to Israel to meet the rest of the delegation and return with them in time for the Opening Ceremonies.

Our arrival at Munich's Airport would have been entirely inauspicious except that Andrei's contagious excitement had no limit. Even after the massacre, in the days of my darkest despair, I had to smile when I thought about his enthusiasm to be a diplomat. I close my eyes, and I can still hear him laugh.

****

"Do you believe this?" my dear friend exclaims as we disembark. "We are here! And do you know what I'm gonna do as soon as I can? I'm gonna find an athlete from Lebanon and give him a big hug, tell him how glad I am we get to meet at the Olympics where we cannot be enemies. It's against the law of the Olympic truce. A dream come true!"

I laugh because I know that Andrei is right. We are in a sacred place, and we are here to commune with the world's best athletes and to create for the next two weeks a perfect world of harmony and peace through athleticism.

A greeting committee, sent to the airport by the German Olympic Committee to welcome us, is here to escort us to the Olympic Village, and it makes me nervous that we are so visible. Everything about being an Olympic athlete is visible, and I am naturally a little shy. But I follow Andrei, who is decidedly not shy, as he throws himself into the arms of one of the officials and walks arm in arm with two of the greeters to our waiting van.

As we are escorted to our quarters, a local band follows, playing Hava Nagila. Andrei puts his arms around Yehuda's and my waists and sweeps us into an impromptu hora. We all hug one another and continue on our way.

Walking around the Village, I keep wondering who I am, as I feel I am a stranger to myself in a faraway world, experiencing a level of happiness I didn't know was possible. The leader of our greeting committee tells us that the Village has been designed to accommodate 10,000 athletes plus the staff needed to keep everything clean and operational, all the athletes well fed and comfortable. But we are among the first to arrive, and we are alone in the Village except for a few locals testing the facilities, a skeleton crew of support staff and officials. We have arrived in Valhalla, and we have the whole place to ourselves!

My skin tingles with the excitement of it. I can't believe what I am seeing. We have entered a major suburban complex – so many buildings in all sizes and shapes, crisscrossing roads and sidewalks, a man-made river whose concrete banks are lined with newly planted trees and shiny chrome picnic benches. Swimming pools, Ping-Pong tables, sunbathing areas beckon us; there's plenty of room for 10,000 athletes and their guests and assistants to spread out and enjoy the moments when they are not competing. I want to partake of it all.

"Look," Yehuda points out. "There's an underground highway that connects us to one another. This place is fantastical!"

Beyond the walkway, neatly arranged in easily accessible fashion, are shops and amenities of all kinds: sports emporia, cinemas, restaurants, hair salons, souvenir kiosks, fresh vegetable and fruit stands, news counters. Everything you could find in a small city is here for our convenience.

Andrei cannot contain himself. "Look, boys, at all the flags! The whole world will be here, and we will all be brothers!"

I must admit that I, too, am overwhelmed by it all. It's a perfect nearly-autumn day, and a multitude of flags, every color in the spectrum, sparkles beneath a lapis lazuli sky freckled by wisps of winter-white clouds. Surely I will explode.

"You will notice," explains our guide, "that the streets are named for famous Olympic athletes."

We have come to the designated Israeli Delegation house, Number 31 Connolly Street – Connollystrasse – after James Connolly, Irish-American track star, called "the first American champion of the modern Olympic games," who won the triple jump and medaled in two other events at the 1896 games.

"Look Yehuda, "I observe. "Our house has multiple entrances. And see there? The door to Apartment 1 will never be locked because it is connected to the parking garage. How are they going to guard a building that has so many ways in?"

"Ssh, Dani. I'm sure they have a good plan. Relax."

The place looks like a modernized version of those massive apartment complexes that sprang up all over Europe after World War II. There are tall houses, short houses, sprawling houses and petite ones. Ours is one of the smaller multi-stories, and that seems right, as we are one of the smaller delegations at the Games. But it is odd to see that our four-story dwelling has five entrances, five doors, all painted blue.

Andrei punches me lightly in the belly. "Look over there, Nervous Nelly." He points to the dining hall. "See that? Our place is almost right on top of the dining hall. You'll never be far from your next meal!"

I inhale deeply, and as I do, I notice the unmistakable odor of coffee – Turkish coffee at that – in the air. Some of my tension eases. Food and drink are always a source of comfort.

Our hosts point out the 10-story building directly across from us and tell us that the East Germans will be staying there.

"Hey! It'll be like having the largest team of body guards in the world, wanna bet?" Andrei is laughing. "No kidding. By the time they've checked in they will have counted our doors and will have taken pity on us, so they'll adopt us on the spot."

We enter, and I see that while the place is institutional, it is also very comfortable, well equipped with everything necessary to make us feel welcome and encourage us to feel at home. Each of the five doors enters into a duplex apartment, and the names of the athlete-occupants will be displayed on the doors that lead into the domiciles.

"Well, I still don't see why they are putting a team from Israel in this building where the security is less than impeccable."

"Will you cut it out, Dan?" says Yehuda. "After all, we are protected by the Olympic truce."

Andrei slaps me on the shoulder. "Look around you, Schatzi. Here are only peace, love and light."

Ever the student, Yehuda chimes in, "Of course you know he's right. Let me remind you that the Olympic truce is a very old tradition – all the way back to the time of the first Olympics, in the 8th Century BC."

I know. In that year, the King of Elis invited athletes from all the kingdoms around his, in what is now modern Greece, to compete in the Ekecheiria, a series of athletic competitions and celebrations to last ten days. He mandated that from the seventh day prior to the opening of the games until seven days after closing ceremonies had been celebrated, all conflicts must cease so that athletes, artists, spectators, anyone interesting in participating in any way, could travel to Olympia to participate in the Games and then return safely home. From that day forward, Olympic athletes have been expected to come to the Games without politics. There is no agenda but the innocent conflict of athletic opposition.

"Okay," I laugh, bumping Andrei with my hip. "Let's get checked in and get this party started!" Yehuda hooks arms with both of us.

"Now you're talking, my friend," he laughs happily. Andrei stops, unlocks his arms from Yehuda's and mine and faces the two of us.

"Which apartment do you two bachelors want for your pad?"

"What do you mean?" I am astonished. "I thought we were all rooming together."

"Don't be silly," Andrei retorts. "Two young bucks sharing an apartment with an old married man? What would the neighbors say?" He pauses. "Besides, Ankie would kill me."

I look at quiet, studious Yehuda and think to myself, "Andrei's nuts." But I won't oppose him; we will live in separate quarters.

"Which flat do you like, Yehuda?" I ask politely, though I already know where I want to be."

"You're kidding, right?" Yehuda giggles. "They all look exactly the same."

"Okay, then. I choose Apartment #2."

"Why?"

"I have no idea. I just want to be in that one."

"Well, that's fine for you two," declares our coach. "I'm taking #1. It's the only one with steps that lead down into the garage. See over there? I like that. I can sneak in and out, and no one can tell Ankie what I'm up to."

"I think you're being ridiculous, Andrei. It'd be so much more fun if you'd just come with us to #2."

"Nope. It's settled. I'm moving into #1." He picks up his bags, and we hold the door and look inside as he saunters into the doorway. After he is swallowed up by the darkness of the entryway, we carry our things to apartment #2.

"Whew, Dani, you two are really insane. Andrei should have come with us, but we could have gone with him. Look at this."

He's right. This apartment is pretty much identical to the one we just saw Andrei go into. Each one is a duplex that is entered by a main door. On the ground floor is a common room with a television and a couch, a small kitchen – everything very functional and modern, clean if not cozy.

"True. But I really want to be in #2. It feels right." Yehuda nods blankly. He's not going to argue. We continue our inspection of the premises.

To the right of the kitchen is a flight of spiral steps leading to two bedrooms. Each room is designed for two athletes. At the top of the stairs, one bedroom faces the pavement of Connollystrasse, and the other faces the balcony, overlooking the garden. Between the rooms is a large bathroom.

"Who's up there?" Yehuda points toward the third and fourth floors.

"Didn't Herr Schiller say the Uruguay and Hong Kong delegations are up there? I know I heard him say they reserved the penthouses over Apartment 4."

"That's right." We continue our inspection, and I am calmed by the memory of something else our guide had told us. "We've got a caretaker living on premises, and we have a steward just next door."

Climbing the stairs to our room, I cannot help but notice that the wood slats squeak miserably. "This is not good, Yehuda. How am I gonna get in here after the parties are over in the middle of the night without waking you up?" Yehuda laughs at me and hits the back of my head with his cap.

We have chosen the room with the balcony. The front rooms are noisy, but the garden below the balcony keeps things quiet.

"This is great, Yehuda. I can bring food out here to snack on, and we can sit outside to drink and smoke."

"You can sit outside to drink and smoke," Yehuda grins. "I'll just watch..."

"Hey, Yehuda, look at the size of this closet! I'd 've brought more stuff if I'd have dreamed we'd have so much space to keep stuff in."

"That's great. But what I like is that the glass doors open right out onto the balcony. I like the aroma of flowers better than the way you're gonna smell after practices!" He blushes. Making a joke doesn't come naturally.

****

Neither of us had any idea my choosing this apartment would save both our lives.

In that pre-dawn rape of our happy-ever-after, the Palestinian terrorists invaded Apartment #1. Even after he was wounded by a gunshot to the head and was bleeding profusely, Moshe Weinberg was ordered to lead the assassins to the rest of the Israel athletes' quarters. He led them out onto the pavement, past Apartment #2.

Why he led them directly to Apartment #3 will remain a mystery, though we have all speculated that he might have thought that wrestlers and weightlifters were more evenly matched with Kalashnikov rifles than two fencers, a speed walker, two small-statured marksmen and a team doctor. In any case, none of the fedeyeen seemed to notice or to care, and as soon as he had taken them to Spitzer's apartment, Weinberg made a last attempt to overcome his captors. They shot him in the chest and threw him out onto the pavement where he bled to death.

For years, every effort I made to tell my story was erased by the thought of dear Monye leading those killers by our door and moreover by the marauding image of his body flattened on the pavement, drowning in that torrent of his own blood.

It's hard, too, because I have such lovely memories of our time in Munich before that Black September morning. When we returned to Tel Aviv for the weekend between our pre-Games practice with the German team and the Opening Ceremonies, I was able describe the village and to entertain Yoram, my younger brother, who was also a great fencer with Olympic hopes of his own.

****

Despite the disruption, I was at least somewhat glad to be home. I was grateful for the opportunity to share with my family, to tell my father about the Olympic Village and make it more real for him, so that when he watched the events on television, he could picture the proceedings more vividly. I had photographs and mementos, and I hoped to make him feel more like he was a part of things. Still, selfish as it made me feel, I wished they had let us just stay in Munich and have us meet the rest of the delegation there. I shared this with Yoram one night.

"If it were up to me, Yoram, I'd still be there in Munich with my milk bar girl."

"A milk bar girl? Is she the reason you look so pudgy, brother dear?"

Embarrassing. He was not far from right. My milk bar girl was certainly part of the reason I had gained six kilos since I had left for Munich two weeks before.

"She's delicious, brother, but she doesn't get the credit. You would not believe the food in the Olympic Village!"

We were extraordinarily fortunate where food was concerned. It was superb, abundant and free. Everywhere I went there was another delicious delicacy from another country, and I could not resist the exotic tastes and textures, rich and sumptuous desserts, infinitely flowing wine and beer. The mood there was inevitably joyful.

"Aren't you fencing?"

"Every day, twice a day. Long workouts."

"Then I guess you're eating late into the night."

"Well, it doesn't take all that much time. Especially when I have the limitless bliss of the frozen delights at the milk bar and the doting attention of the milk bar girl."

"I know you love ice cream!"

Do I! I have always loved ice cream, ice milk, frozen yogurt – any way you prepare it, any way you serve it, if it's a milk product and frozen, I cannot get enough. So the milk bar, provided for us gratis by the Olympic Village, was a treasure trove I dared not dream of. And the beautiful young woman who presided over the shop, a cerulean-eyed, creamy- complected Austrian volunteer, was my constant companion, my Munich heartthrob.

"Especially when it's served by a Viennese beauty!"

"Are you in love, Dani?"

"No. Not love, Yoram. But this girl is fun to be with. Every evening we go to the pubs in Munich – the locals insist that the beer is much better than it is in our Village. I am not sure if that's quite true or fair, but I love hanging out in those pubs. We get to know the local people a little, and they love celebrating with us. We sing folksongs, shoot pool, and dance till late in the night. I go to sleep exhausted, and then I can't wait to get up so I can repeat the pleasure of the day before."

"What're Yehuda and Spitzer doing while you're out carousing?"

"You kidding? They are my other constant companions. I don't know if they love the ice cream as much as I do, but they eat their shares, and they seem happy with the daily routine."

"When do you find time to practice?"

"Easy. We begin early in the morning with a skirmish against the German team in the small hall near our apartment, and then we go to breakfast, which is the first great event of the day. After that, we go to the Fencing Arena and work out again before and after lunch, and afterwards, our evening frolicking begins.

"It's unbelievable, Yoram. Every day new athletes arrive, and there are more and more languages spoken everywhere we go. Andrei is funny. He has taken to inviting the Lebanese and the Syrians to join us. You should've been there. The first time he invited them, Yehuda said to him, 'But Andrei, they are our enemies.' 'Not here!' Andrei insisted. 'Here we are not even separate nations. We are athletes, opponents in a noble rivalry. That is all. How many times can I tell you this?' We never see him frown, even when one of us makes a mistake in practice."

"Good thing you're going right back. You don't want to miss any of the action."

I had to laugh then. I don't believe there ever was a lull in the excitement. As more athletes arrived in the Olympic Village, the nightlife became more exciting. I especially loved the Village disco, where they had good and inexpensive beer and a large dark smoking area around a stairway. That's where all the smokers congregated, athletes inhaling cigarettes, giving each other permission to share this forbidden pleasure. Everyone knows that the most interesting people in the world are the smokers, and I always wanted to be with them. Knowing that I was among very elite athletes who were also smokers gave me incredible pleasure.

"You know what I especially love, Yoram? I especially love hanging out with the Americans. They're the true hipsters."

"Perfect. You've been practicing your James Dean walk as far back as I can remember."

"Only since I was 13."

"Good thing you can blow those fantastic smoke rings that just hang up there in the air, and you wear the right kind of blue jeans. I bet the Americans think you're 'awesome.'"

"Sure. Andrei and Yehuda are always making fun of me. When my milk bar girl is not with me, I dance with everyone. Anyone!"

It's true. One night I asked a girl to dance, and when she stood up, I could see she was at least two heads taller than I. I felt so short and pudgy I wanted to run under a table and hide. But I danced with her, and we had a great time. She was Ulrike Meyfarth, a West German high jumper!

Yoram laughed aloud. "Good thing my training is going well. We'll take the Olympics by storm together in four years!"

"Yeah. That'll be fun. Montreal's supposed to be a really groovy city too."

"Do you really use those dumb English words?"

It was hard to tell Yoram everything – there was so much going on, and even when there wasn't, it was fascinating just to watch the people.

Some nights Spitzer, Yehuda and I just stood around while the other athletes interacted with one another. Tall ones, small ones, round ones, flat. We made a game of guessing the sport of each athlete just by measuring him or her with our eyes. What made the game more intriguing was that you could never tell what most athletes were thinking. What is that word? Inscrutable. They are inscrutable, and they don't share their feelings openly. Not in an Olympic Village anyway.

"Dad said you were in a hospital?"

I had to think for a minute what he was talking about; everything the family knew, they only knew in bits and pieces. It was so hard to communicate from the Olympic Village.

"Yeah, but not because there's anything wrong."

I had had the honor to be chosen to participate as a subject in a very small, selective study. A group of doctors gathered some of us in the hospital every day in order to record our reaction times, our speed and agility, our resting heart rates and lung capacities, our overall health. I was among gymnasts, swimmers, water polo players, runners, wrestlers, the crème de la crème of world athletes. So when the doctors announced that I was one of the fastest athletes in the Village, I could hardly believe it.

"When you think about it, it's really rather amusing. Me. Faster than the sprinters! Imagine that."

"I'm not surprised," Yoram said solemnly. "You can't fence your way to the Olympics without being fast on your feet and as strong as a shot-putter."

After a mere two days in Israel, without even time enough to adjust to the time difference, we were on our way back to Munich, and Andrei was even more animated than before.

Andrei Spitzer had been a good fencer in his day, but he always thought he would be a better coach than a competitor. He liked teaching, and he was really good at bringing out the best in others. He traveled to The Netherlands, where he attended a school for coaches, and there he met and married Ankie. When Spitzer returned to Israel with his bride, they moved to a border town called Biranit, near Lebanon, where he founded a fencing school. The Israeli Olympic Committee chose Spitzer to coach the '72 team because of the enormous success he had had as a coach, and now Ankie was on her way to Europe so she could take their daughter Anouk to meet her Opa and Oma in Helvoirt, The Netherlands.

Instead of accompanying Andrei to Munich, Ankie and Anouk flew separately to her hometown, where she was planning to leave the baby so that she could return to watch our events unencumbered.

When we arrived in Munich, our women athletes and our sole sailor checked into separate compounds while the rest of the male athletes returned with us to Connollystrasse 31, where the weightlifters and wrestlers chose Apartment 3.

Yehuda, Andrei and I helped everyone else get their bags out of the van into the apartments, and Andrei accompanied us to Apartment #2, where we were joined by Henry Herschkowitz and Zelig Shtruch, both marksmen, and by speed walker Dr. Shaul Ledany. We pleaded with Spitzer to move into our place, and the marksmen asked the same of their coach Kehat Shorr; we assured them that they'd be happier with us. But both declined. Shorr, the other coaches and the referees went on to Apartment #1, but Andrei hung back, reluctant to leave us yet. All three of us seemed to want just a little more of the special, exclusive intimacy we had been sharing.

Spitzer, Yehuda and I were overwhelmed with the changes that had transpired here in the Olympic Village, where everything was more hectic than it had been when we left just three days earlier.

"Look at all these people!" Andrei could not get over the diversity of humanity surrounding us. "The place is overrun with delegations!"

"Yeah," I snarled. "Athletes swarming all around the grounds. No more space for roaming around. No more instant gratification at the bars and restaurants. We're in for long queues wherever we go."

"Oh, Dani. You're just miffed because you'll have to wait your turn for your milk bar girl."

Secretly I was grateful that the pleasure factor would be diminished. It was time to concentrate on the serious business we came here to do. Time to concentrate on the swords!

The day before the competitions began, Yehuda, Andrei and I alone among the Israeli Olympians made a pilgrimage to Dachau. I was astonished that more of our teammates were not along, but Andrei was philosophical.

"Oh, you know," he said thoughtfully. "Most of them just can't face it. Like Tuvia Sokolovsky, the weightlifting coach? He was in a camp. Shaul Ladany and Yossi Romano too – Yossi's mother didn't want him to come to the Olympics at all; she's been having nightmares that the Nazis would finish what they started. And then there's Kehat Schorr – he was in the Romanian resistance and lost his wife and daughter. He told me he just can't bear to go near the camp. Some of the others are children of survivors. So it's up to us to go and represent everyone."

At the camp gates, we were met by a group of Jews from the local synagogue.

"Whew, guys. Do you believe all these people came back, chose to live here again, after what the Nazis did to them?" I remember being struck by how poignant it was that it was Andrei Spitzer, normally so blithe, who posed this question.

"I don't understand it either," Weinstein muttered. "How can anyone want to live in a country that so deliberately hurt them and their loved ones?"

There was no explanation, but what was clear was how proud and happy the community was to have us there. No Israeli flag had ever before flown in an Olympic Stadium on German soil, and I thought we must have been some kind of just retribution for them."

An old woman from their group lit ceremonial candles, and on her wrist I recognized the tattoo of the camp prisoner.

"Shema Y'Israel," we all sang together. "Adonai elohenu. Adonai ehad." (Hear O Israel, the Lord our God is one.)

Overcome with emotion, Andrei whispered to me, "Schmuel should have worked harder to get more of us here. It would have meant so much to these people."

"So true," whispered Yehuda. "These are our family, not strangers."

I nodded, and we laid a wreath on the monument before we left.

"You see why we're here, boys? We have so much to be grateful for." Andrei Spitzer declared, blowing a kiss to the woman who lit the candles. Then he waved and shouted at the villagers, "We'll keep in touch. You are in our hearts, as we are in yours."

We floated through the Opening Ceremonies, and then it was time for my competitions. I didn't do as well as I should have, but later, with hindsight, I could see I had no reason to complain.

"Okay, Dani," Andrei said to me right after the opening ceremonies were over; "It's time to buckle down. You couldn't be readier."

"I agree," I nodded. "I can't wait for the fencing to begin."

My first bout was an easy win. My opponent was ranked #5 in the world, but Andrei was quick to remind me, "Look, you already beat him when you fenced in Paris. And guess what? He's the top-ranked German fencer, and you know how much the Germans love fencing, right? This bout is gonna be televised all over Europe. You'll be a star."

It was an exciting match because the top tier of German politicos was in attendance. Hans Jochen Vogel, the Mayor of Munich, Gustav Heinemann, the President of the Republic. The crowd sizzled with the expectation of gold.

A fencing arena is normally a very civilized athletic venue. The spectators usually sit in neat rows, and they hold their hands in their laps, their heads moving back and forth as they follow the action on the piste(specially marked rectangular area for fencing). They call out their support in subdued voices that rarely reflect the true tenor of their excitement.

But this fencer and I were very closely seeded, and our records were very similar. There would be little of the customary decorum in that match.

"Now just breathe, Dani," Andrei coached me. "You have superior skill in psyching out your opponent. Besides, when you fought him before, he taught you everything you need to know to stay ahead of him."

But the fans did not know this. And since most of them were German, and because the Germans held most of the international fencing titles at that moment, all expectations were that the German fencer would score his five hits quickly and effortlessly.

Being the fencing fans that they were, however, they were delighted to find that the bout was going to make them sweat.

"Don't even think about it," Andrei encouraged me when my opponent managed to score the first hit very early in the bout.

The assembled crowd applauded politely, and the German officials clearly enunciated congratulations to my opponent above the growing hum of German affirmations.

Ankie's voice soared above the rest; I was glad she'd arrived in time to see me fence. "Stay focused, Dani."

"He's got a hit," I heard Andrei shout before I realized I had. The crowd lost its equilibrium. Now all I heard was a jumble of noise, and Andrei, Ankie, the Munich Mayor, the President and all disappeared into the din.

"You're doing it, Dani!" Andrei screamed. "Now you're gonna show them all a real competition!"

The suspense was short-lived, however, because in very quick succession, I scored my next four hits, and the bout was over. I was declared the winner.

Andrei and Ankie took me out to celebrate. "You'll be famous, dear Dani," crooned Ankie. "Your photograph will be in all the German newspapers tomorrow!"

"Yeah," laughed Andrei. "And the bout will be shown over and over on all the German television stations!"

"Good," I giggled with excitement. "Maybe one of the international broadcasters will pick up the transmission and show it in Tel Aviv. Then my father could catch some of it."

My next three opponents are a bit of a blur. I fought an Italian fencer, an Irishman, and the Cuban National Champion, and I beat them all.

In the next group, I scored victories over the Czech fencer and the Argentinean fencer, and I was on my way to the very top. Until I faced a British fencer by the name of Bill Paul.

"Okay, Dani," Andrei advised before the bout; "You are a technically better fencer than Bill Paul. Your footwork is more adept, your sword positions are more precise, and you've got more incisive timing. That may not be the whole battle, but it should give you the advantage."

"Don't worry," I replied confidently. "I'll be out on the piste with an opponent I know well. I cannot fail."

Our spectators were fairly subdued. They seemed resigned to the fact that I would win, that this would be a very uneventful competition with no drama to speak of. I clearly had the upper hand, and there seemed to be no surprises in the air.

While I fenced, Andrei spoke softly from the sidelines, and I could hear him. Ankie's deep voice impassively intoned over and over, "Nice work, Dani. Keep it up. Bring it home," and the like. Before long, all I could hear was the squeaking of my shoes on the piste, the clinking of the swords as they met, the buzz of the electronic scoring machine when I got a hit. The air was calm, and I thought to myself, "This one is going to be easy."

In no time, I got to four points.

"Yup, this'll be over in no time," Spitzer told his wife. "I'm going out for a soda, and when I get back, Dani will have already won."

Then, suddenly, everything changed.

The British fencer stopped abruptly and asked for a break. I was astounded. How could I know what was going on with him? I wonder now if it was only meant to confuse me, and if that was his goal, he succeeded. Was he having a mental breakdown, I wondered? Was he succumbing to a nervous attack? Before I could figure it out, he was back on his feet and saying he was ready to go. Then he fenced furiously. I lost my momentum, was totally off my guard, and he got up to four points faster than I could count them. Without even working hard enough to breathe heavily, he beat me by slamming out the fifth hit.

I was devastated. How could this have happened?

Suddenly it was all over. I was eliminated! My competition was over. Just like that.

"I don't get it, Andrei," I almost pleaded with Spitzer after the bout "I prayed for this win. God has never let me down before."

Andrei studied my face for a moment and then laughed at me. "Well, my friend, either you have offended God and lost His favor, or maybe it's just that Bill Paul's Jewish too. Maybe your prayers just bumped into one another, and yours got knocked out. Or maybe his connection is better yours."

I was inconsolable. Then Spitzer reminded me, "Listen, Dani, 10,000 athletes came here to compete in the Olympics. Only 1,000 will leave with medals. That means that 9,000 athletes will leave with no medals. Will those 9,000 take memories that mean any less than those of the winners? I doubt it. The great accomplishment is that you were here at all."

"You're right," I admitted. "To come here, just to be in this place, is to have ascended to Heaven."

"Exactly. So let it go now. Let's get drunk and dance. Next week you'll be back in Tel Aviv training for Montreal."

Ankie agreed with her husband that we all needed to have some fun. "We'll cheer you up, Dani!" So the three of us grabbed Yehuda and headed for the disco.

At the HofBräuhaus, Ankie made me her special project. She was determined to see me smile. "Dance with me, Dani," she demanded. And we did dance.

We danced one dance after another. We danced a lot, and we danced wildly. I have always been a good dancer; it's part of my success as a fencer and has a lot to do with the fact that I'm a musician too. I love to dance. So I didn't want to stop dancing any more than Ankie did, and we danced until late into the night.

"Andrei doesn't look happy, Ankie," I pointed out from the dance floor at one point.

"Don't worry about Andrei, Dani. Just dance. He's probably too busy making world peace to notice."

But Andrei could be a very conservative guy, and he had become jealous. I neither knew that about him nor could have anticipated it, and by the time we stopped dancing, he was all worked up.

"Did you have to dance so close, hunh, Dani, did you? You can't find a woman of your own? You need mine?"

"You're being ridiculous, Andrei. Leave me alone."

"You apologize, you creep," Andrei screamed at me. Ankie came between us.

"Don't be an idiot, Andrei. You're acting like a fool."

She dragged him back to her hotel, but he didn't speak to me for two days. Even though I knew it had to pass, I was very hurt. Still, it did make me stop feeling sorry for myself over losing my bout with Bill Paul.

I met Yehuda, who had also been eliminated by then, back at our apartment and told him, "I hadn't realized till tonight how very young you and I both are. Especially for fencers. There will be other Olympics."

"Right, Dani. Perhaps we'll both be like Henry Herschkowitz and return till we're gray. This is just the first of many Olympic Games for us!"

I knew that I had let myself be thrown off balance by a strategy I had never seen before and that I had learned a valuable lesson. I vowed to concentrate on training for Montreal when I got home.

"You're so right, Yehuda! And now, let's go to the Olympics!"

And that was that. I turned my attention to seeing the other athletes at work. I was lucky beyond imagining in my acquisition of tickets. It was nearly impossible to get into the swimming and gymnastics competitions, but I consistently managed to get into both.

I saw the American Mark Spitz win three of his seven gold medal races. The experience of the swim meet is so different from a fencing tournament. Those fans are wild, uncontrolled in their frenzy; they paint themselves, wear costumes and hold banners with wild slogans. Even the swimming itself is very dramatic. In every heat there are surprises – swimmers in far-flung lanes out-touch the top seeded swimmers in the center lanes, and every fan in the stadium is on his feet screaming and jumping up and down. With the Spitz competitions, the excitement was augmented by the fact that he was breaking records by breaking records. No swimmer had ever swum to so many first place finishes in any Olympics, and even his opponents were rooting for him at times. I have always loved swimming, but the way Spitz did it there was like a perfect, liquid song flawlessly sung. I felt honored to have witnessed his victories.

I was absolutely awestruck by Olga Corbett, the little wonder from the Soviet Union. She was a gentle love poem in motion, scoring a perfect 10 on the balance beam, which was not even her first perfect score. While the fans' approval resounded over the blare of the music in the floor competition arena, the thumping on the pommel horse, the rhythms at the parallel bars and the clink of the rings, I cried. Truth is, I actually wept. Every sinew in that little girl's body was flawless in its slightest shrug, every minute tilt of her head or tiny motion of her hand created a body symmetry, a balance I'd never imagined. I learned a lot about what I might do to work my body more efficiently by watching her. She never wasted a single breath or the merest effort. Every centimeter of her being was in sync with every other. She moved me deeply.

But my luckiest achievement was getting tickets to see the match between the Soviet Union basketball team and the Americans. A basketball venue has a life of its own. Even in Munich, away from the commercialism of the American arena, there was a sense of the business of basketball. Advertisers' banners were everywhere, professional scouts kept everyone on edge, and fans were just insane. Horns and trumpets, drums and noisemakers competed with the Jackson Five soundtrack pumped over the loudspeaker. When the teams entered, and the fans went wild, yelling, booing, cheering, throwing confetti and streamers and popcorn till ushers instructed them to cease, and that set the mood for the entire game.

This was a match-up that shocked the world, too. Who could have predicted the Soviet victory? The Americans then were so cocky, so sure victory would be theirs. They believed winning to be their birthright. Since 1936 when basketball became part of the Olympics, the Americans had always won. Maybe there was some political power the Russians used in the tournament, but I know basketball, and I saw that the Soviets played their hearts out. They won because they had the skill and the teamwork to win. It was humbling just to be there.

Andrei and I fixed things between us, and then he went with Ankie to Helvoirt, her hometown in The Netherlands. He told me he had to go because, "Ankie just told me she's been keeping a secret – she didn't want to ruin my enjoyment of the games. Can you imagine?"

"What kind of a secret, Andrei?"

"Our little Anouk has been in hospital – I told you Ankie's brother is a pediatrician there in Helvoirt, right? He thought it would be better for the baby to stay in hospital until the Games are over so Ankie wouldn't have to worry."

"That's scary."

"Yeah, but she's much better, and Lalkin's given me permission to spend a night with her there. I'll be back in 24 hours."

And so we parted company, and the next night I went with the other members of the delegation to see Schmuel Rodenski in Anatevka, the German language version of Fiddler on the Roof. After the show, we were invited to visit Rodenski backstage, and we went to take a lot of photographs.

The show was delightful, which I had expected. After all, every Jewish kid knows Tevye, the Sholem Aleichem milkman, and this was with such beautiful music.

After the show, exhilarated by the performance and exhausted from my day's activities, I went back to the Olympic village to await Andrei's return from The Netherlands.

When he arrived, Andrei's spirits matched mine. He had brought some risqué magazines for my father, and for me some luscious Dutch chocolates that I immediately devoured. Within moments of his arrival, we were laughing heartily. Being with Andrei was always such fun.

"Ah, Dani. I am glad to be here with you now, but I must tell you, I didn't miss you for a moment."

"How's Anouk?"

"Mmm, much better. By the time I leave Munich, she'll be home and waiting for me so she can vomit on my shoulder again. You cannot know, Dani, how she pleases me. I never knew you could love any tiny little person this much, could get so much pleasure just from looking at another human being. I never imagined being a father could feel so fulfilling."

"You're just an old softie, my man." I remember feeling just a little bit envious of his happiness. But then he told me a story that immediately sent chills down my spine, a story that haunts me still.

"Last night, before we went to sleep, Ankie and I resolved that we'd catch the ten o'clock train from Den Bosch station so I could be back in Munich early enough to get a good night's sleep. This morning, Ankie got her brother's car, and we were on our way in plenty of time. But I couldn't leave! I just could not bear to leave little Anouk without seeing her one more time, without holding her just once more.

"Ankie scolded me and said she'd have to change the driving route to stop at the hospital, and she warned me we might miss the train. 'What would be so terrible then?' I asked her. 'I'd just have to spend another night with you.' You know how serious Ankie can be. She gave me one of her looks and said, 'Andrei, darling, you gave them your word you'd be back tonight.' 'Don't worry,' I assured her. 'Just drive.'

"So she detoured to the hospital, and waited in the car while I ran in and gave my baby a hug. I raced back, and even before I was safely in my seat, she gunned the engine; we were off to the train station.

"Of course, the train was gone. But it had just left. 'Look here,' I said. 'I'll just call them and tell them I'll come tomorrow.' My wife was not amused. 'Andrei, you know I'd love that, but you would be miserable. You gave your word.' She was right, so I told her to drive to the next station.

"Ankie sped to that station too, and there the train was just pulling out as we drove up. 'Listen,' I instructed, 'Try one more station. If we don't make it, I'll know it wasn't meant to be, and I'll just stay on with you.'

"This time when we got to the station, the engineer was just calling, 'All Aboard.' I jumped from the car and chased it down. Once I was on, Ankie left the car where it was and ran alongside the train yelling, 'I love you, Andrei.' I wanted to cry. I yelled at the top of my lungs, 'I love you too, my Ankie.' And I do."

Andrei smiled and popped a chocolate into his mouth. "You know what?" He spat chocolate, talking while he chewed. "I wish I kissed her again before I got out of that car."

****

When I was a youngster, my father told me, "Never run after a train, a bus or a girl. Relax, and let life bring you your aim naturally. Destiny always has its way."

****

In 2009, I visited Shmuel Lalkin in his retirement home. As he strode to meet me in the lobby, I was struck by what a figure this man cut. At well over 6'3", he still stood nearly straight and towered over everyone. His boundless energy lifted his every step, and he seemed far younger than his nearly 84 years.

"Dan Alon. It is good to see you," he enthused as he sat with me. Despite a frustrating chest and head cold, he was anxious to talk with me, to reminisce about our experiences in Munich.

"You're writing a book! Wonderful. There are two people in this home who are writing books, and I'm for all of them."

"Ours is the only one that will be published in the United States."

"Good, good. There can't be too much written about it. Too many people don't know what happened in Munich."

"True," I said. "Especially the young people. They know nothing!"

Later, as I was about to take my leave, Lalkin leaned in close to me as though he were about to tell me a deep secret. "Listen," he said, looking around to see if anyone was listening. "I want to tell you something you probably don't know."

Lalkin's story made my heart stand still.

"At that time, my son was a bar mitzvah. Thirteen years old. And he said to me, 'Daddy, I want to go see the tennis' – he was a very good tennis player – 'so as a gift why not take me to the Games with you?' So I asked my wife, and she said, 'All right. You know what? I'll go with you.' So I took a flat from a family in town – you could rent rooms in people's homes – and they came with me. That night when we all went to see Fiddler on the Roof with Shaul Rodenski, I brought them both, and after the show, some of the wrestlers approached me and said, 'Mr. Lalkin, your son is a fan of ours. We are his heroes. We would like to invite him back to spend the night with us in the Olympic Village.' I looked at my wife, and she shrugged. 'You decide,' she said. So I said 'No.' My son was only thirteen, so he began to cry, and I told him to go back to his room with his mother. I don't know if he cursed me or not, but he was very angry, and for him I was the devil. The wrestlers, too, begged me to relent. 'Please, Mr. Lalkin. It's just for one night.' But I said no again. All my life since then, I ask myself why, but I don't have a reply. Perhaps I thought because I was the Head of the Delegation it was inappropriate? I don't know. Really. I just said 'NO.' And it is for that reason that my son is a doctor today." He paused and then continued wryly. "He often reminds me of this."

Later, I saw that Lalkin's story is in Aaron Klein's book, and in front of it, he said the same thing, "I told no one." The story must rest like a bad dream in his head, a dream he wants to believe he never truly experienced.

CHAPTER 3

Aftermath

"Why is it the Jews' fault? Because it's the truth."

    Rudolfine Robinson

"The Israelis were faulted for their intractable refusal to release Palestinian prisoners."

    Aaron Klein, **Striking Back**

A few seconds before leaving Munich

When I returned from Munich, my expectation was that I would recommence my training. I thought that after we all recovered from the shock and the wrenching pain, life would just pick up where it left off. I couldn't have known the name for it then, but I am sure I suffered from post-traumatic stress syndrome, and everything I tried to do seemed to fizzle in my hands.

Returning to anything close to normalcy was painful and difficult. No one ever asked me how I was, if I was recovering, if I needed to talk about anything. Unlike Tuvia Sokolsky and Gad Tsabari, who actually escaped from the besieged rooms, those of us in Apartment 2 were considered outsiders. We were not perceived as survivors but rather as some kind of interlopers, former athletes who just happened to be in Munich at the time of the massacre. I had no words to articulate this sense that I had that we should have died or at least been injured if we were to get some recognition for our pain. The families of the dead victims, even the terrorists got more attention than we did.

The truth is that even if I were asked, I could not have described the anguish, the despair that haunted me in the aftermath of the Games. I was, in many ways, paralyzed.

At first, I attempted to return to my routines, which meant practicing with my brother Yoram. Yoram had always been a source of solace for me, and I believed that being with him would ease the suffering.

Yoram was born six years after I was, and from the beginning, he was a calming influence on me. He took after my mother, where I was definitely my father's son.

The first thing my mother noted after I was born was that I had my father's hands and physiognomy; soon thereafter, she said I had his temperament, and she was right. Dad was a high strung perfectionist, often nervous and agitated, too serious, impulsive in his reactions; he had a short fuse. I was not as ponderous as he, but I had to work at relaxing. My father could seem almost manic, as he was as intent on having a good time when he was playing as he was on succeeding when he was working or competing. I was that way myself.

My mother was patient, kind and calm. She hated fencing because of the turmoil it created in our lives; there were the tension of the competition, the drama of the politics, the constant upheavals, and she detested them. She sought quiet tranquility, and Yoram took after her.

Yoram had the ability to look at any situation objectively and to take his time, considering all sides, before he was likely to act. He tended to be phlegmatic, unflappable, which made him a great fencing companion and an even better business partner, which he was – our business was one of the leaders in the packaging industry for thirty-six years, thanks to his cool head and my ability to get things done. It was like God created Yoram to be the perfect brother for me, and it was a special blessing that not only did he like fencing, but also that he was very good at it!

There were two outstanding facets of Yoram's fencing that made him my ideal partner. One was that he was left-handed, which meant that I was never in a position to be facing a left-handed opponent unprepared. I regularly fenced against right-handed opponents in local matches, and I had Yoram to keep my on my toes against a southpaw. In addition, Yoram and I had a special ability to communicate wordlessly, to read one another's actions and anticipate each other's moves. This came from the fact that when he was learning to talk, I was the only one in the family who could understand him. We had a kind of language that was ours alone, and we became entirely tuned into one another's thoughts.

When we went to competitions, we were also able to collaborate to influence the outcome of a match. This is a practice that fencing teammates often engage in, and we were especially good at it. In a league competition, the fencer with the most victories is the winner of the series. When we would both reach the final round, we would team up against the other team, combine our strengths to beat the other club. If he would win, I would lose my chance and vice-versa. If the opponent was more formidable for one or the other of us, we would "give up" the match so the other could take the big win. This is commonly done in world or international competitions, but it's difficult to achieve in local matches if the partners are not as well matched as we brothers were.

Our relationship extended to our social life as well. I would date a girl for a while, and then he would date her. We often dated the same girl at the same time, and we more often went on double dates. Yoram didn't marry till he was 43, which drove my mother crazy – she didn't live to see him marry as a matter of fact – so for much of our lives we went to discos together, went on vacations together, shared hotel rooms when we went to fencing competitions, etc. We practiced every day with our coach and ourselves, and we shared many friends among the other fencers. It was always a lot of fun.

So after Munich, it should have been soothing to have immersed myself in my fencing. But there was always the nagging reality of the Munich Olympics tugging at my equilibrium. At first I couldn't work at all, couldn't bring myself to go back to work in my father's business. I took Valium, tried to take an interest in things, but I had no heart for business, no heart for fencing. I was entirely dysfunctional.

Yoram had been keeping me company, taking care of me, actually, since my return from Munich. He had been, in fact, staying with me, even sleeping with me in my big bed because I was unable to sleep alone. We were bachelors, of course, and that meant that we were pretty lax about putting our clothing away, and it would often pile up on the chair in the bedroom. One night, the chair became so heavy with the clothing that it gave way, falling over onto my brother, wakening him. He jumped away from it and bumped into me. I began to fight him, pommeling him with my fists, screaming at him, all the while he was yelling, "Dani, it's me, Dani, it's your brother. It's Yoram." But I kept crying and punching him until he turned on the light and pushed me down. That's how fragile I was at that time.

There might have been resources, experts who might have helped me, but I was under the radar because I had merely gotten away and as such people perceived me not as one who got away, but one who was simply, albeit miraculously, overlooked and therefore in no need of consideration for trauma I could not have experienced. It soon became apparent that I would have to help myself, to find my own cure.

It so happened at that time that Maestro Berger, a new coach, had recently arrived in Tel Aviv from Russia. I went to where he was working and watched him; he was a good coach. Though he spoke no Hebrew and I no Russian, we managed to communicate, and soon we were working together. We worked very well together, and I found that I wanted to fence again because I had in Berger someone I felt I could trust. Through fencing, I thought, I would re-interest myself in my life.

Along with me, Yoram was ranked among the top six fencers in the country, so it was natural that he would once again become my fencing partner, and we began to train under this new coach. Berger recognized my experience and my potential and decided to re-teach me everything I knew. He wanted to eliminate my mistakes. He changed every move. It was very hard, but I trusted him. I felt if I continued, I'd be in good shape for the October '72 International competition in Israel for the big Judeah Prize. Fencers come to this event from all over Europe, and I had won it twice already before the Olympics. Berger expected me to attend this competition with a degree of confidence because of my talent, and I had the same expectations because I knew how truly improved I was.

I did win. And I won easily. Yoram took third place. We were absolutely confident that we could develop and do well in the Montreal Olympics together. We were optimistic, and we made our plans to go to the European championships scheduled for that spring in Paris. Every evening my brother, my coach and I would practice, and we were more than ready to take this one on.

In advance of the European championships, I was invited to France to train with the French fencers for three weeks prior to the competition. It was a remarkable honor to be offered this opportunity. The Israeli Fencing Federation said I must go, and, of course, I was excited to do so. Yoram would come with me, and we would stay at the Rassing Club, a very exclusive place; in prior years, the club had excluded Jews from staying there, and now we were to be their guests not only as Jews but as Israelis. We would be two of over two hundred international fencers, an elite contingent of the best in the world.

My brother and I met with the Israeli fencing officials and asked what kind of security would be provided.

"We are sorry, Dan and Yoram," they answered. "There is no budget for security."

Well," I replied. "We won't go without security."

There was a very uncomfortable silence between us. Then I said, "Why not send us only for one week, and then you can use the leftover money to pay for security?"

They said no, that would not be acceptable and told us we must accept the challenge from the French and spend the entire three weeks training with their team.

"No," I said resolutely. "We refuse to go unless we have security."

The delegation visited my parents.

"Mr. and Mrs. Alon, you know how this looks. Your son's refusal to go to Paris as planned gives power to the other side. It wouldn't be fair to Israel if we were to surrender to terrorism; that would enable the enemy to win."

We didn't see it that way. My father had a bad heart, and I was not about to make him worry. Again I insisted on having some security; again the committee said no.

I took my case to the Head of the Israeli Sport Federation and to the Minister of Education and Sports. Both told me this was not in their jurisdiction. However, the Fencing Federation had acquired a new delegation member, who was instructed to come see me.

"Dani, I am very angry with you."

"You have no reason to be. I am only asking what is right."

"You must do as the committee asks! You owe it to –"

"Owe? What do I owe? To whom? I was in Munich, and I saw what happened because security was not a priority. I won't put myself in such jeopardy again."

But the delegate was unmoved and said simply, "If you and Yoram won't go to Paris, I will personally see that your career is ruined."

I held firm. The committee sent two other fencers to the competition, and they went without security!

Two months later, the Maccabiah Games were to take place in Israel. The Maccabiah Games is a huge completion that is held every four years in alternate years to the Olympics. We put the Paris affair out of our minds and practiced for the Maccabiad. A month after Paris, however, I saw an announcement in the newspaper that Yehuda Weinstein, who was ranked number 2 or 3 behind me, had been chosen to go to South Africa for a competition instead of me. The Federation didn't even have the decency to call me to tell me I had been overlooked.

I called for a press conference, and in front of my beloved country, I announced that we would both quit fencing. The journalists went to the Federation and asked them why the Alons were leaving their sport, and the Federation lied and said that we had asked for too much money. Of course we had asked for nothing; this had become a dirty business.

Eight years later, I went to South Africa with my wife, who was from Johannesburg, and my three children. While I was there, I visited a local fencing club and met with the club president.

"Do you remember about eight years ago you sent an invitation to Israel for a fencer to come compete in South Africa?" I asked the President. "Did you mention a name when you made the request?"

The Club President shook his head. "I asked for the Israeli champion. I wanted them to send the best fencer in Israel, that's all."

I simply nodded; the president had substantiated a suspicion I had had all along. When the Head of the Fencing Federation had told me they were sending Yehuda, they told me it was because the South African officials had specifically requested Yehuda Weinstein.

My fencing career was over, even as I was poised for victories at Montreal and beyond. In the end, I was grateful that I neither competed in the Maccabiah Games nor traveled to the match in South Africa. Even at home in our own arena, the Fencing Federation didn't place so much as a fence around the athletes to guard against invasion, and in South Africa I doubt we'd have been protected. Nothing happened, thank God, but the possible dangers were infinite, and I would have been unable to concentrate on the fencing.

****

Turning my attention to my private life, I returned to my business and focused on starting a family.

I was ready for a new kind of life, a new set of challenges, and I was no longer so afraid. Somehow, standing up to the committee and then severing the tie to fencing liberated me to pursue other facets of my persona. In my youth, I had had other great talents, other passions besides fencing, passions I had had to lay aside in the quest for the Olympics. Now that that dream had been charred, I looked into my past for keys to my future.

When I was in Kindergarten, my talent for painting was discovered, and it was a source of great pride for my father. Twenty years later, during the time of my military service, I went to visit the Kindergarten I had attended, and the teacher remembered me immediately. She introduced me to the class, and as they applauded, I realized that some of my work was still on her wall, now framed. Later, she explained that whenever they had an art project, she would point to my pieces and remind them that they had a high standard to live up to. When they did something especially well, they would boast to one another, "I am painting like Dani! I will be the next Dan Alon!" Now that I had left fencing, I thought perhaps I would take up painting again.

Additionally, I was a fairly accomplished musician, absolutely mad about music. My classical musical education began with my mother, who took me to the Israel Philharmonic when I was 12 to hear the Mozart Clarinet Concerto. As soon as the soloist began to play, I knew I had to play the clarinet, and my parents were delighted. I took private lessons once a week, and my teacher, who had played in the Opera Tel Aviv when Placido Domingo was in residence there, assured us all that I was very talented and should continue to study and practice.

So I did. I played the clarinet every day before I went to fence; then I would study and go to parties. This was my routine throughout my school years. I loved making music as much as I loved listening to it; I played in the school band and traveled to musical competitions almost as frequently as I traveled to fencing competitions. This was my life until I reached the age when I was old enough for the service.

When it came time to join the military, I auditioned for the army orchestra with the Mozart Clarinet Concerto. The orchestra was very selective and only took a limited number of musicians; I was chosen. Unfortunately for me, another clarinetist was chosen as well, and there was only one clarinet chair available. There was going to be another round of auditions just for the two of us, but I saw that he was really far less physically suited for the military than I, and to my ear he seemed the better musician. So I withdrew my name from consideration. From that day on, I never touched the clarinet again, I am sorry to say. Nonetheless, I know that my sensibilities are defined by the fact that I have the eye of an artist and the ear of a musician.

The fencing association attempted to arrange a non-combat military role for me, teaching fencing on the base, but I rebuffed the offer, preferring instead to be sent for training as a paramedic. I soon concluded, however, that I would never be able do that. I was absolutely unable to stand it. Perhaps it's my artist's sensibility, perhaps it's just my weakness, but since I was a child, I had no tolerance for blood. I vomited when I pricked my finger! At the base, I went to my commander and asked for a transfer. He laughed and told me to get used to it.

From then on, I made a concerted effort to fail at my exams, which were administered every Friday. I wanted my commander to think I was an idiot, even though I knew all the material very well. Because I was "failing," I had no permission to leave the base on my weekend off. One Friday morning, after our weekly exam, a parachutist with whom I was friendly and who was authentically failing, challenged me to go with him to Tel Aviv for the weekend. I wasn't all that adventurous at the time, so I declined the offer. He pressed me, and though I knew it was terribly illegal, I finally agreed to go. We hitchhiked into Tel Aviv, and I was home in time for Shabbos dinner.

My parents were furious with me when I explained to them what I had done. My father ordered me to go back immediately, but now I was feeling frisky. Instead, I spent the next day at a fencing competition, and I won. We returned Sunday to the base. Right after I got back, I was summoned to the commander's office. I knew that if I didn't have a good story, I would surely go to jail. Before I could take a breath or think it through, I was standing in front of the commander, and he was asking me where I was all weekend.

"I was right here, Sir," I lied.

"You never left the base?"

"No, sir, I was studying for our next test."

The commander was pensive for a moment, and he squinted his eyes looking at me long and hard.

"That's not true," he finally said. And before I could protest, he said he had read about my bout in the newspaper, so he knew I was in Tel Aviv! I had no defense, and I was headed to the brig. But it actually worked out okay in the end.

We went to court, and I managed to stay in the corps rather than being mustered out. If I met certain specified requirements, my time in jail would be minimal, and I met those conditions easily so that I only served seven days. For three months after that, I was not allowed to leave the base, not even to go home. I went back to the paramedic school and never failed another test. The best part was that when I finished the course, they sent me to the Air Force to be trained in bombing operations. I spent a year in active duty and then entered the reserves until I was called back to active duty two or three weeks before the 6-Day War. I remained on active duty until the 11th of June, the day the war ended, at 8 a.m.

Serving during the 6-Day War had a profound effect on me. Because I am a Sabra and because the birth of Israel was such a personal event for me, I was deeply moved by the change in the way Israel was perceived as a result of the war. Suddenly, we were no longer just a group of stragglers, an inferior fighting force composed of weakly Jews; by beating the Egyptians, the Syrians and the Jordanians in a single sweep, we had lived up to the image of King David the Giant Killer and had become winners. The perception of myself as a Jew and a warrior contributed greatly to my strengths as a fencer.

After the Paris affair, when I was re-evaluating my life, I saw that I could easily turn a corner and use all my experiences, which had made me a well-rounded individual with many contrasting strengths and an acute propensity for introspection. I was ready to settle down.

Settling down was a new concept for me. As quiet and as careful as I always was, I surprised myself with my ability to party. From the time I was a teenager, I had been very social, and because of fencing and music, I had had a wide and somewhat eclectic circle of friends. A real rock'n'roll fanatic, I lived for Friday night disco visits. I would find myself wishing that our

Shabbos dinners would go quicker, would wolf my food down and be as cordial as possible with my parents, but as soon as I could get away, I was off to meet my friends.

This was, after all, the early 60's, and we idolized American music in Israel. I adored James Dean and Elvis, and I looked a little like a young Sal Mineo, so I developed an acutely American fashion sense. I owned the perfect American-style blue jeans, wore my high collars starched so they stood stiffly around my neck, I and never went anywhere without my leather jacket. My dark hair was slicked back with brill cream, and I smoked unfiltered American cigarettes that I kept in the pocket I formed by rolling my t-shirt sleeve and which I lit by striking a match against the sole of my shoe. Because I looked so good and yet was polite and seemed shy, I attracted the women quite easily, and I had many girlfriends, with whom I would dance the nights away. I loved how their hoop-skirted crinolines would undulate as they danced. On Saturdays we would congregate together at the beaches, which I loved because of the party atmosphere and the multitude of bikini-clad women.

I found now that I missed that happy-go-lucky self, the one who inherited from my father a fine-tuned joie de vivre. But by this time I was 30 years old, and I certainly was not about to revisit the disco scene. No. I needed to find a good woman with whom I could enjoy life but with whom I could create stability.

And just when I was thinking I should begin my search in earnest, I met Adele.

Yoram and I were driving home from visiting a girlfriend I had in the North one evening when we saw this beautiful blonde woman standing by the side of the road, hitchhiking. From the moment I saw her I was her willing victim! I told Yoram I would stop for her, and he should let me do all the talking because I was going to make her my girlfriend. Yoram didn't agree, as he found her attractive as well, but he got into the back seat, and we competed with one another for her attention all the way to her apartment. She spoke no Hebrew, so we were all speaking English, and I was quicker than he was in getting down to business. When we got to her destination, I told her I would take Yoram home and be back in an hour to take her dancing.

"No," she said, emphatically. "I'll give you my number, and you can call me."

"Tonight we'll go dancing," I insisted.

"What's the hurry? " She laughed. "I'll be here, and you can call me.

"It's now or never, Miss. If you don't come out tonight, we never will."

She accepted, and a month later, we announced our engagement at a pizza party with my parents. Unfortunately, my father died one week later, so he knew I was about to be married, but he missed the wedding, which we then postponed for six months. When we did marry on June 16, 1977, we had no music, no dancing, just the Rabbi and a few people.

My bride's name was Adele Goldman and she had come to Israel from South Africa all by herself, without the aid of family or friends, with $50 in her pocket. She had grown tired of an awkward, difficult situation at home in Cape Town – her parents were divorced and contentious, so she had been sent to multiple boarding schools, had been cared for and educated by many strangers but not by her own parents – and she came to Israel to make a new life. She took a job as a secretary and rented an apartment in the city; when I fortunate enough to encounter her on the road, she was on her way back from a Rosh Hashanah visit with family outside Tel Aviv.

It took such courage for her to come to Israel that way! Even though she longed to create a completely new life of her own, actually doing it was anything but easy. Like most people who make aliyah, she had heard and read about Israel, but the factors that compelled her to immigrate overshadowed the fact that the intelligence she'd gathered painted a disarmingly inadequate picture of what lay ahead for her.

Her South African background was very conservative; she had had no television, no real connection to popular culture until 1968. In her home country, Apartheid was still in power, and the government was repressive. Israel was everything that South Africa was not – liberal, both politically and socially, very open, free. The first thing she had to learn when she got to Tel Aviv was how to immerse herself, to harden her personality, to drop some of her genteel politeness.

It was very difficult for Adele in the beginning. People's abrasiveness bothered her, and the struggle to find a professional path would have been daunting to someone with less conviction. But she was very strong, very independent, and she knew what she wanted; she was also determined to succeed at whatever she tried, and she had no doubt that she preferred the challenges of Israel over the easier life she had left behind in South Africa.

Adele understood what I was able to tell her about Munich, but I will admit that that was something I never fully disclosed. I still didn't know how to talk about the experience. I just wanted to forget it. So, at age 32, I asked this wonderful woman to be my wife. I became my father, the consummate family man.

Before Adele was 27, she had borne me three beautiful children Meir, named for my father, Arik and Pahzit. Each was, in his or her own way, the apple of my eye, and I doted on them. I must admit I have always had a special softness for my daughter, but I adore all three. And I was very happy that I could bring them up without the stresses that had plagued me. In truth, I never told them about Munich. They knew I was there, and they knew there was a massacre, but we never really talked about it. In fact, my family never saw me fence.

For twenty years, I stayed away from fencing except to coach youngsters in a country club in Tel Aviv. No one except the pupils themselves realized who I was, and my connections to the Federation of Fencing in Israel were entirely nonexistent; I coached as a hobby, without passion, as a service. Then, when I was 47, I was approached by some of my pupils who had now reached their twenties and wanted to prepare to fence in the national championships. They begged me not only to teach them but to fence with them as well. "We can learn so much from fencing alongside you," they said. "If you are there with us, we will surely prevail." So I was convinced.

By this time, the emigrations from Russia had brought many fencers to Israel. These Russians didn't know me, and I didn't know them. They were stunned when I won the competition. So was I, and moreover, so was my family. This was the first time my wife or my children had seen me fence, and they had no idea I could win. After the competition, my middle child, my son Arik decided he would like to take up fencing, so I agreed to teach him.

Arik was small for his fourteen years, but he was determined. We practiced together, just as my father and I had done, and he progressed enough to win the Junior Championship, just before he enlisted in the army. After he left the army, like many Israeli children do after they finish their military service, Arik traveled for several months, visiting South America, Spain and Thailand; he certainly wasn't fencing. Upon his return, he enrolled in the university and only returned to fencing much later. He has since won the Israeli National Championships, making him the third generation of Alon men to do so.

An interesting side note here is that Arik might have been another Olympic contender, but he chose to concentrate more on his future as a writer and a filmmaker than on competition. It's no longer possible to fence and study and work and fence, as it was when I was young, and he needed to look to developing his career options. I think he made the right choice, even if it means he never had the chance to go to the Olympics. Even now, as I tell my story, I realize I would not feel safe sending him.

It could happen again.

****

The paralysis that plagued me after Munich persisted for years, and even after I had regained equilibrium, had put 1972 into a perspective, had begun to share my experiences with the Games, I could be stymied by it without warning. I would be involved in something that seemed entirely removed from that awful day in September, and suddenly, I would be grabbed by a flashback that would throw me into a panic.

In 2006, I went to Berlin to talk about Munich to the Jewish community there, and they sent someone from the congregation to pick me up at the airport. They took me to a lovely little hotel, and when I walked in, I suddenly went numb. The receptionist was speaking Arabic, and the manager of the hotel was an Arab as well. I tried to be calm, tried to be open-minded, but I could not catch my breath. Finally, I walked to the synagogue, which was nearby, and I found the rebbe there. "Rebbe," I practically cried. "I came here to speak about Munich. I can't stay in a small hotel that is operated by Arabs. Please, find me a different hotel, something large enough to have other customers I can easily identify as my own people. I will never be able to sleep in that place." The committee understood and immediately moved me to a different hotel.

The same thing happened again that year when I was in Aspen. The group that had flown me in to talk was going to meet in the reception room of a beautiful 19th Century hotel, and they decided I should have the very best accommodation the hotel had to offer. They assigned me a bungalow in the forest. It was gorgeous, had a Jacuzzi, skylights, a feeling of complete calm, and if I had been there with my wife, it would have been very romantic. But I was terrified. It was out in the woods, exposed to the world, with no one around for what felt like many dark miles. I was too terribly alone in it, and I could not stay there; I was petrified with fear. Again, they had to move me because even then, 35 years after the horrors of Munich. I could not feel safe anywhere that remotely resembled Apartment 2 at 31 Connolly Street in Munich. Whenever I fly or take a train or any transportation other than my own personal car, I feel the same terror, and I literally hold my breath until I reach my destination.

I have reinforced my memory of the place a few times now. The first time I returned to Munich was in 2002. I had gone to Germany on business, and by chance I had found myself for one night in Munich. In the evening, after I'd concluded my business, I decided I must visit the Olympic Village and see for myself what it was like thirty years later. I flagged a taxi.

The driver was unfamiliar with the address I gave him, my address in the Olympic Village, so I had to guide him there as best as I could. He was very nice, and we struck up a conversation.

"What is it you're looking for," he asked me.

"I'm just returning to see where the Munich Olympics happened in 1972."

"Oh," he said, looking at me quizzically. "What was that?"

I had forgotten that there are people all over the world, even in the town where it happened just as in my own hometown of Tel Aviv, who do not know what took place at the 20th Olympiad here in Munich. So, while I guided him to the Village, while I directed him how to go under the pedestrian way into the parking lot near our building, I had plenty of time to tell him the story. He was riveted, and when we arrived and gazed into the pitch darkness that surrounded us, he said, "I will not leave you here. I'll wait, and when you're ready to return, I'll take you back; if you need someone to just stand near you, I'll be that guy too."

I went to the pavement and stood as I had on that miserable day, staring at the entrances to the apartments that now house students. There was a sign next to the entrance to Apartment #1 that said simply that in 1972 these were the buildings that were home to the Israeli athletes who were killed in the Munich Massacre. I could not move for a full twenty minutes; as I stood there, it all came back to me, and I thought I would faint.

Why did I choose Apartment Number Two? All the others preferred apartments One and Three, yet I was adamant that we fencers be in Number Two; no one could sway my opinion any other way. Was I guided by the hand of God? It felt that way all these years later. Why else would I have been so stubborn? At that moment, I felt grateful, and then I was overcome with an anger I had been unaware of until that moment.

Why did the officials or whoever chose this building for the Israeli delegation insist on our being in this particular location? It was totally unsuitable. There were no gates, and it had five easily accessible entrances. The lock on the door was so inadequate that any mildly strong wind could open it. In the absence of a fortress, why was there no guard to protect us? I began to tremble, this time indignant with rage and with ire rather than with fear. I think that that is when I finally began to feel some peace return to me. I felt less guilty and less responsible as I remembered that I had warned everyone not to leave us there. And I was not the only one to have done so.

Like me, our Israeli Head of Delegation Schmuel Lalkin had inspected the compound in advance of the Games. He protested vehemently against our being left there in that building. He pointed out the easy accessibility, the lack of security, the vulnerability of the location, and he said over and over again that it was unfit for Israeli athletes. He went back to Israel, and he wrote letters to both the International Olympic Committee and the German Olympic Committee, and he wrote to the Israeli Olympic Committee. All of them decried his accusations, swearing that the German government had taken all precautions to ensure that every athlete would be safe. In the end, realizing that they would not listen to him, Lalkin requested that the athletes at 31 Connolly Street be armed. "I asked them that I, at least, in Apartment #5, be allowed to have a pistol. 'At the very least,' I begged, 'a pistol.' They laughed at me. The Germans told me to 'mind your own bloody business.'"

Remembering this in 2002, I knew I had a new mission: to be the shaliach, the messenger. I see it as my duty to tell the world that they failed us, and unless they are vigilant, unless they heed the lesson, others will suffer as we did.

****

I'm retired now, from business as well as from fencing. I travel for pleasure, not for business, and I enjoy my family – my wife and my three grown children. My son Arik is now married, and I look forward to the day when I will be a grandfather. I like to think that if I have grandsons they might dream of and work toward the Olympic games as fencers, but I want to know that they will be safe, that the world will take note of what we learned in Munich.

The subsequent Olympics have been far safer, to be sure, and there is an abundance of security everywhere you go these days. But I don't know that the fundamental root causes of the terror in Munich has been completely embraced, completely understood, and I hope that my work as the shaliach will illuminate some of the underlying truths that enabled the world to be so lax about the Twentieth Olympiad so that it will NEVER happen again.

****

A person born in Israel knows a lot of sadness. It is just a fact of life that one's days will be colored by tragedy. Yes, there have been moments of pure elation, utter joy, as I felt at the Opening Ceremony of the Olympics, on my wedding day, at the births of my sons, especially when Pazit, whose name means "pure light," was born in the very same hospital where, twenty years earlier, my grandmother had died. But in every period of my life, I have also known great tragedy. In Kindergarten, my best friend died of polio. Later, in high school, another best friend died of a brain tumor. I lost many friends in the war, but still another best friend died during the war of typhus from bad drinking water. Still, though I learned to live with loss and mourning already as a youngster, nothing prepared me for the way I would be traumatized by the Munich Massacre.

CHAPTER 4

In My Father's Court

"In winning his medal in 1936, (Endre) Kabos added to a long tradition of Hungarian Jewish excellence in fencing. Between 1908 and 1936, Hungarian Jews won an astounding total of eighteen medals in this sport. Austro-Hungarian Jews zealously took up fencing in the late nineteenth and early twentieth centuries in order to defend the "honor" from anti-Semites."

*David Clay Large, **Nazi Games***

Meir Ufalvi, first from right, with his team in Hungary

Meir and Blanka Alon with Dan at approximately age 3

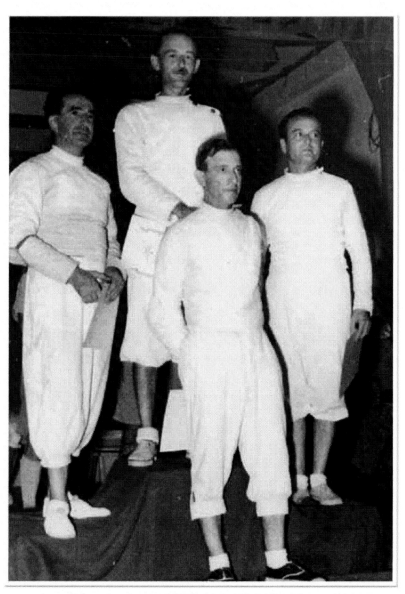

Israeli fencing team, 1953. Meir Ufalvi first from right

I never ever wanted to be anything but a fencer. That is, if I ever did dream of anything else, I certainly have no recollection of it. My earliest memories are of my parents' kitchen, surrounded by the aroma of Turkish coffee, olives and fresh bread and by the sound of my father and his fencing friends arguing with my mother.

My father was never able to sit for any length of time; he seemed to be forever subconsciously advancing and appeling, always envisioning himself on the piste where he taught me the basics. My father taught me everything important that I know about life.

When I was three years old in 1948, Israel was brand new. We lived in Tel Aviv, where the constant bombings reminded us incessantly of the jihad to eliminate our homeland. Once, our home was hit.

I remember standing in the smoke-filled night, clutching my father's hand, waiting for the soldiers to tell us that it was safe to go inside our house. We were all unharmed, but our house was a shambles. I wanted to go somewhere else to live, to take my family and fly up into the sky, get on a cloud and burrow into its folds where no more bombs could find us.

"Listen, Dani, my kisfiam," Abba said to me. "Life has very few rules. But this I know: there are some things you can control, some you can't. And when you can't steer the boat, you jump. If you are not willing to accept that, you will never be a winner. Right now we are in a boat we can still steer. The best thing to do is to stay and face the wind."

In those days, my father belonged to a fencing club, and I have very strong memories of Abba returning from a fencing practice or a bout, standing in the kitchen, in that utterly erect manner of his, his center of gravity never faltering, washing his hands, wiping them, preparing for the meal for which his sessions would work up an appetite.

"The saber is a mighty weapon, édeskisfiam," he would tell me. "But nothing is as mighty as your own heart. I would not be alive today if I had relied solely on my sword."

So many times at that kitchen table, he told and re-told the story of how he came to be in Israel. Born Meir Ufalvi in 1916, my father grew up in Budapest, just as all of Europe was beginning to become a very dangerous place to be. The War to end all Wars had merely whetted the German appetite for conquest and destruction, and all over Europe, among the vanquished German allies, the enemy had already been identified: The Jew.

"But I had nothing to do with that, Danike. I was a boy, protected by my family's love and indulgence. Once I fell in love with fencing, so long ago, I hardly noticed anything else until I was all grown up."

My father was a very athletic boy who had tried and succeeded in gymnastics and in swimming. But no other sport captured his imagination. An early injury nearly robbed him of a hand, and as soon as he was healed, he discovered the powerful draw of the saber's pommel, and immediately the sword had him in its grip. He was smitten.

The love of fencing, my mother was wont to remind me, came naturally to him. "Of course he loves the sport," she would say. "He is Hungarian. A Hungarian Jew to be sure, but Hungarian to the core. Ask him what that means."

Of course, she was right. It's not unusual that a Hungarian boy should dream of fencing. My father took great pride in this. "Did you know, Dani, that the Hungarian cavalry invented the saber? Oh, sure, the Italians popularized the sport of fencing and changed the design of the sword, but we Hungarians perfected both."

Hungarian Jews never really believed they were any different from the cultured Hungarians. They were thoroughly assimilated in a civilized world, and they had a passion for the sophisticated Hungarian culture. So of course they had a passion for fencing – many of the world's greatest fencers were Hungarian Jews.

The men my father admired from his youth are bigger than life in my own imagination.

"I had such heroes in those days, Dani," he used to tell me. "So many great fencers in our circle." I especially loved when he would talk about his fencing idols because soon he'd be recounting the story of Endre Kabos yet again.

"No one was like him, Dani. No one. I saw him fence so many times, and he always amazed me.

"I was 17 when Kabos won his third European championship in a row, and the club where I practiced held a party to celebrate. He came to the party, and I tell you, Dani, if I had been a woman, I would have fallen in love with him there and then. Nothing is quite so sexy as a human being who burns with his kind of passion. Especially one with his kind of talent."

Endre Kabos was the most celebrated fencer in the Austro-Hungarian world and a member of the most decorated fencing team in all of Europe. Till 1935, Kabos and the Hungarian team dominated European fencing. Kabos went to the Los Angeles Olympics of 1932, when he was only 26, and he won two gold medals. Four years later, at the 1936 Olympics in Berlin, Adolf Hitler himself presented Kabos with the gold medal for saber fencing.

Between competitions, Kabos worked in his grocery store. He was not rich, and he had no patrons, but he loved his sport, and he loved his country, so he worked hard to glorify them both.

"He was everybody's hero, not just in the Jewish community or even just in Budapest or Hungary, but all over Europe. To show their appreciation, the Jewish community gave him a special trophy for his achievements, for the way he represented us in the world." Here my father would sigh. "I was following in Kabos' footsteps, Dani. I was not far behind him."

Meir Ufalvi had placed very well in his European bouts, but he didn't qualify for the Olympics of 1936. He was really too young; fencers do not usually ascend to their peaks in their youth like some athletes do, but rather require maturity. Instead he set his sights on the 1940 Japanese Olympic Games.

By 1938, everyone agreed that Endre Kabos would pass his torch to my father Meir Ulfavi. He had won the Hungarian national junior championships that spring, and he was nearly finished with his textile engineering studies at the Budapest Technion. He was scheduled to begin an internship and to go to work in a textile mill immediately after graduation.

Plans changed, however, when Papa found himself in Zagreb, Yugoslavia, for the European championships. In the middle of the competitions, he received a telegram from a friend at the university. "Do not return to Hungary," the message warned; "Not Safe!"

The Austrian Anschluss with the Germans was complete, and Jews had been declared aliens in their own country.

At that point, he really wasn't sure what to do. He said that he wanted to believe that his family would be all right, that they would know that he was alive and well, but he could neither send nor receive messages. He sensed that to go back would mean certain destruction and saw no other way but to abandon his saber and run.

"For years I hurt deep inside, thinking I had left my friends and family in Budapest, believing I had failed by not going back to help them, but I didn't let my emotions govern my actions. There was too much to do."

In Zagreb, Meir discovered the Jabotinsky movement.

Before Zagreb, Father already admired Ze'ev Jabotinsky, founder of the Irgun, the militant Zionist movement in Palestine that built steadily, attracting European Jews in large numbers as the Nazi discriminations escalated. All over Europe, but especially in Yugoslavia and Poland, young Jews involved themselves in the effort to topple English rule in Palestine and make it a Jewish homeland. Jabotinsky warned the Jews in the 1920's that Eastern Europe was rife with anti-Semitism, that the Land of Israel was the only hope for a viable Jewish state where Jews could shed the threat of Jewish homelessness. He was outraged by the hunger, the abject poverty that engulfed Eastern European Jewry, and he was determined to create a country that belonged primarily to the Jews.

My father really threw himself into the movement. He worked as a courier, as an arms trader, as a driver. Every day he put his life was on the line, but the Jabotinsky ideal kept on pushing him. After three months, he finally got to Palestine.

Father often said that he felt like he left every part of his old self behind in Europe, so in his new land he needed a new name. He chose to be Alon, for the native Israeli tree, which, like an Oak tree, grows strong and straight but is flexible in the wind. With his new name, he joined the Haganah.

Once upon a time, Haganah was just a small Jewish guard, a kind of vigilante force that protected farmers from Arab vandalism. But by 1938-39, it was already a national force, a reserve army of guerilla soldiers always prepared to attack and topple the British and Arab power.

Finding a way to feed himself and pay the rent while he volunteered in the Haganah proved to be a great challenge. Even though he had nearly graduated from the Technion with a degree in textile engineering – and he never failed to mention that he was at the top in his class – he could not find a job in Palestine. There was literally no industry, no work in textiles. He took a series of odd jobs and survived. And whenever he could, he practiced his skills in the graphic arts.

Abba found great pride in his work. "People were amazed by what I could do, Dani; they said I made letters and illustrations like the calligraphers of those illuminated manuscripts I showed you in the Beth-Hatefutsoth." But there were no jobs in the graphic arts, so Father had to settle for what he could get.

After he settled in Tel Aviv, Papa got a lucky break. He went to work as a tree painter, painting citrus and other trees – trees that were unaccustomed to the desert sun – white to protect their barks from burning. This apparently made my father very happy. He was making enough money to live without fear, and, most importantly to him, he was free to find a club and return to fencing.

Meir learned to love what he had in Tel Aviv. If he ever regretted his choice to abandon Budapest, he had no luxury for self-pity. He was busy surviving. And soon it became apparent that he had made the only real choice that was viable. It was the fate of Endre Kabos that confirmed his gratitude for that fateful telegram.

When the Nazis arrived in Hungary, they went immediately to Novgorod, where Endre Kabos lived, and took him to a concentration camp. Kabos was actually lucky to be in that particular camp because a Hungarian guard in the camp recognized him and helped him to run away. He could have gone right then to America or to Palestine, someplace where he would be safe from the Nazis. But Kabos made a different choice.

Instead of leaving Hungary, Kabos sneaked back into Budapest and joined the underground. He trained to work with the demolitions experts in the resistance, and he immersed himself in the struggle to oust the Nazis from of his beloved country. Nothing mattered to him so much as making Hungary safe for all Hungarians.

One night, driving a truck loaded with explosives on a bridge at Magrit, the bridge that separates Buda and Pest, the two parts of the city, from one another, Endre Kabos' luck ended. His cargo exploded, and he died.

"We all choose our battles, Dani," my father never tired of telling me. "And our lives take us where we are meant to go. Just like Kabos, I did the right thing."

"But," my father loved to remind me. "I also realized after the war that it was time to put my faith in something even more substantial than fencing. I needed to find a wife."

In those days, Palestine was still a British mandate." The European Jews were tired of the British, wanted no more foreign rule. But, paradoxically, the British actually made Jewish lives rather pleasant, especially in Tel Aviv, where there was no limit to places to go to listen to live music, any night of the week, to dance in dozens of clubs. Most of the new émigrés had left sophisticated lives in Europe and were grateful to the British for the cosmopolitan air of Tel Aviv. The beaches were clean and beautiful, and all around a nearly forgotten sense of leisure and merry-making pervaded the city.

According to both my parents, they had a "glorious courtship," as my mother would effuse whenever given the opportunity. "Every day at 5 p.m. the beachfront cafes and restaurants served high tea, we could sit for hours just to listen to music, watch citizens dancing the rumba, the tango, the jitterbug. Sometimes I could convince myself I didn't miss Vienna, that I didn't worry about my parents, that I didn't even think about Hitler."

Tel Aviv was an urbane locale with all the amenities. Abba had many friends, most of whom were refugees with low-paying jobs or no jobs at all, but their mood was light because the British sensibility was soothing.

"What always amazed me about the British," my father would often marvel, "was that even though they knew that the Irgun and the Haganah were out to finish them off, they maintained that stiff upper lip. Their morale remained high, and they treated us with respect."

Tel Aviv was a great place to be young and to go courting. My mother, born Blanka Albin, was a primly pretty refugee from Vienna working in the city as a secretary. She met my father at a coffee house in 1941. Her beauty and her cleverness with money made her an ideal match for my father, so when he was ready to open his own business, he made her his partner. He often said that though he could sell Swiss cheese from the moon, he needed Blanka to write the terms of the sale. They married after a brief courtship and moved into a flat in Tel Aviv with Blanka's parents, who'd just arrived from Haifa, by way of a dislocation camp, after escaping Austria.

My grandparents were a Godsend to my parents, especially after I was born in March 1945.

Soon after they were married, a friend of Abba's found him a job in a new textile plant, and he worked very hard, day and night, in order to save enough money to buy a small textile printing plant close to Jaffa. It was dangerous there, with snipers shooting in the street, bullets raining down on Jaffa and on Tel Aviv, just one street away. Bullets were imbedded in all the walls around every street, but my father told me that he never really feared them – everything felt so right. By the time I was born, my father was doing very well. He had his new family, his own business, his fencing."

Meir fenced more and more. So, by the time I could talk, I was completely indoctrinated in two worlds – the world of Israeli politics and the world of Israeli fencing...which, in its own way, was very political. In our kitchen, where so much of our lives transpired, fencing and life were one for us. Father often repeated, "Life might be a struggle for food, for survival, but if I am fencing, I am strong."

I remember with great clarity a crystal moment: May 14, 1948, the 5th of Iyar, 5708, the day when Israel was partitioned.

My mother was cooking, preparing for a party. And she was muttering just loud enough for all to hear, "Politics. It's all politics. Hapoel, Macabee, labor, mapai, maki. Does it really matter in a sport? Since when is fencing political?" I hid behind a chair while she ranted and listened to my father patiently deflect her anger. She hated the politics of fencing.

"Ssh, Blancsike," my father retorted. "They'll be here in a few moments."

"I don't care who hears me."

"They're here to celebrate, not to listen to your criticisms."

"You're right. Of course. So let's stop talking about it now."

"Exactly! Today is not about factions in sports. Today is about our country, our own country."

Mother's eyes smiled then, but her mouth didn't quite follow suit. "This discussion is not over," she said, grabbing for the last word.

"I know, dragam. But not now."

A sharp whistle distracted all attention. A special high-pitched whistle -- three short shrieks, three longer ones. No melody. Clearly a signal. The signal.

"They're here," Abba announced.

A man's voice in shouted Hungarian reached us from the street below our flat. "Meir. Open up. I've brought the wine."

"Alon. It's me," shouted another. "What's Blanka got cooking up there? I can already smell it, and it smells divine."

My father answered as he bolted down the stairs, two at a time, to open the door. "I don't have any idea what it is, but you can bet it's got oranges in it!" Oranges were the only food we always had plenty of in those days!

"And if we're lucky, some of that black market spam you keep getting from your cousins in the States."

The men on my father's fencing community often came to celebrate holidays. They brought their wives and their children, but to them belonged the presence by which I was enthralled. So powerful were these men, these friends of my father's, that they obscured all others from my awareness.

They were the best saber swordsmen in an elite squadron of athlete/soldiers. Each fencer carried a gift of black market coffee or chocolate. They launched into their celebration the moment they entered our house, and they stayed, smoking and drinking, singing and telling stories in German and Hungarian, late into the night.

Someone asked my father in mock innocence if I could have some barackpálinka, the sweet plum and apricot brandy they all loved. My mother tsikached under her breath, reprimanding the men for suggesting such a thing, worrying about the mess, fussing with the food, admonishing about the noise. When she scolded, she scolded in crisp, every-syllable-enunciated Viennese German, and she left the room every time the political and cultural debates among the fencers, always in Hungarian, heated up. My mother disapproved of all political debates no matter the outcome.

"Politics and other meaningless arguments have no place in my home," she would say. But we all knew as well as she did that her voice fell on deaf ears. The politics of Israel were mothers' milk to these men, most of whom were revisionists, Jabotinsky-ites in their youth, politically astute, opinionated, volatile and absolute. On this particular day, however, there was little debate.

"Turn the radio on, will you Blanka?" one of the men eventually asked. "The announcement's coming any minute now, isn't it?"

Mother disapproved, but she complied with the request. My father fretted over being at home. I remember his saying, "We should be getting this from Ben Gurion himself, in person."

"Oh, no, we're Begin's men. Right here in your house is where we belong."

"Hmpf," sniffed one of the fencers, "Do you really believe that this will make any difference?"

Another shook his head. "The foreigners will still control us, even after we call ourselves independent. Especially the Americans. We have no country without them."

"Are you crazy? Those Americans are just money to us. They don't have..."

"Sssh." My mother cried. "You are making me dizzy with your politics. No more politics. You know what they say: Three Jews, six opinions. You'll never agree, and I'm tired of the debate." The radio crackled. My mother served the coffee and dessert, and the men turned their attention to David Ben Gurion's voice, reading Israel's Declaration of Independence.

The men didn't sit still for long. As they listened their feet came to life as always, moving automatically. Their fingers caressed imaginary sword handles. They stood and shifted their weight, moving their feet to a rhythm in their heads, a rhythm known only to fencers.

At the center was my father, powerful in his court.

I watched and imitated him, moving my fingers to copy the squeezes, skittering my feet to mimic the dancing. Instinctively I moved like my father, with my trunk in sync with my legs, maintaining my center of gravity. At 3, I already knew the simplest footwork, and my feet engaged in an unconscious ballet, forming simple forward crossovers, backward crossovers, half-retreats, half-advances, en gardes.

And all the while, Ben Gurion was making history.

"...We appeal..." I know I don't remember this from that day so long ago, but I have memorized the words since. "We appeal, in the very midst of the onslaught launched against us now for months, to the Arab inhabitants of the State of Israel to preserve peace and participate in the upbuilding of the State on the basis of full and equal citizenship and due representation in all its provisional and permanent institutions."

All the voices were silent but for Ben Gurion's. The static on the radio punctuated the excitement of his words. We all listened as one – the fencers, their wives, we children – our faces flushed with the hugeness of this historic moment.

"We extend our hand to all neighboring states and their peoples in an offer of peace and good neighborliness and appeal to them to establish bonds of cooperation and mutual help with the sovereign Jewish people settled in its own land. The State of Israel is prepared to do its share in a common effort for the advancement of the entire Middle East."

As I remember, we held our breaths. No one seemed able to inhale, so powerful was the effort to simply listen. My father took my mother's hand in his and drew it to his lips. He touched it then to his cheek, and he froze, remaining in that conjured tableau for what seemed like a very long time, as Ben Gurion continued.

"We appeal to the Jewish people throughout the Diaspora to rally round the Jews of Eretz-Israel in the tasks of immigration and upbuilding and to stand by them in the great struggle for the realization of the age-old dream - the redemption of Israel."

All the adults huddled closer to the radio, but in my mind, everyone else melted away, and the only presence that remained was my father's.

Ben Gurion said something about signatures on a paper, and my father's eyes blazed red, tears streaming down his cheeks. I wanted to throw myself into his arms and hug him and tell him it would all be all right, that I'd take care of him just like he took care of me. Instead, he lifted me and pulled me close. "You're an Israeli, Dani. Now you are a citizen of the State of Israel."

Just then, bombs began to fall, including the bomb that fell on our house.

By the time I was six, I begged my father to let me be a fencer just like him, but my father wouldn't even entertain the thought. He said that if I wanted to fight in a few years, perhaps he would teach me. But not yet.

He told me I was too young to fence. "Your hands are not yet strong enough, large enough, formed enough to wield a saber. Or a foil or an epée for that matter. Not yet. I will show you the footwork, and when you have sufficiently grown, then perhaps."

"Over my dead body," my mother moaned. "Another fencer in the house? Why not..."

My father laughed at her, shrinking his small gray eyes into double smiles. "Why make such a fuss now, édes szivem mine?" He was ecstatic that I wanted to fence, despite what my mother thought. He was glad I had caught his passion, and he stood in my way knowing that this prohibition would ensure that my desire to fence would grow.

My mother might have hated fencing and its politics, but my father told me that it was she who caused me to love the sport.

"When your mother was pregnant with you, she would come to all my bouts. She never missed a single one! I used to watch her up there in the gallery, so nervous; she seemed so small, so vulnerable.

"She hated those bouts. She'd keep those intense brown eyes closed while I was fighting, and then she would smile a little, but only when the match was over, and only when I was declared the winner."

I had a lot to live up to. My father was a great fencer. He was the undefeated National Champion of Palestine and then of Israel for nearly 5 years, and he topped countless Europeans and Americans in three Maccabiah games. But he never got to the Olympics.

Palestine had no funds to train and send athletes to the Games, and Father had to be home to take care of business, to tend to his family. By the time I was three, he was too old, and our country was too young. But he was never bitter, never regretful. He looked forward, and he concentrated all his efforts on nurturing me and later my brother as well.

When I was 4, my kindergarten teacher told my parents that I had a talent for painting.

My father was elated. "Perhaps you'll be a great painter, like Marc Chagall, Dani!" He promised to put the work up on the wall as soon as we got home, and he turned to the teacher to say with great pleasure, "He gets this talent from me, you know. He has much more than me, but without me he'd have none. That I know."

When I followed him to his fencing club, he would brag. "Say hello to my son Dani, the artist! You should see his paintings. Next time you come over, I'll show you. You'll see – he could be a big, famous artist someday."

As young as I was, I fully appreciated our bond. I often looked at the calligraphy he did as a hobby and for business. I knew his talent for graphics, and I recognized his reflection in me. I knew that if I were like him in this, then surely I would be like him in all things. He was my father; he was proud of me. And I was bursting with pride in him – he was, after all, a celebrity.

When I was a kid, we had this children's game, a kind of plastic waffle made to serve as a large, multi-picture frame for small likenesses of popular athletes. All the kids collected the athletes' photos and tried to fill their waffles; everyone exchanged photos, swapping extra pictures for those they didn't yet have. The prints varied in value: the less there were, the more they'd be worth. The best part was that when every slot was filled, the manufacturer gave each collector an album made especially to hold the photographs.

I loved my collection. I was the first one in my class to get all the athletes into my waffle. It always surprised me, though, when a classmate would ask me if I had a picture of my father. Of course I did. I was his son. How could I not have him? Some kid in my class once offered to give me his bike for the likeness of my father. I didn't think my father was such a hot commodity. I never thought about it.

"Oh, Dani," my classmates would beg me. "I need that one." Or, I like that one. It's the best." And, Can I trade you my bike for it? If the bike isn't enough..."

I was embarrassed. "What do you mean, 'the best?'" I asked.

"No one has Meir Alon photos, Dani. I asked the man at the candy store why I can't ever find one, and he said it's because everyone wants one. They're worth more than anything else in the collection. You could make a mint by selling them to candy stores."

I was amazed. "You know who he is?"

"You're kidding, right? Know who he is? He's only the best saber swordsman in the country."

Like Hungarians, Israelis love fencing; the saber is especially popular to watch because of the dramatic movement all over the arena, the leaping and cavorting. So my father was a hero to his people, but he was more than a fencing hero to me. He had a great heart, which he revealed to me in many ways.

When I was a boy, my mother's brother lived with us until he married. He served in the Israeli army and was in charge of Tel Aviv ambulances. Every day he drove between Tel Aviv and Jerusalem , and sometimes, when citizens needed to travel from one city to the other, he took them in his ambulance.

One bright, sunny day, my grandfather wanted to go to Jerusalem, so he asked me to go with him in my uncle's ambulance. The old city felt like a cloister where the ambulance was uncomfortably out of place. Inside the walls, in every direction all I saw were wounded soldiers lying on the ground, calling out, moaning. I was stunned, frightened, and I couldn't stay there smelling the blood and the burned flesh anymore. It made me nauseous.

I went outside the walls, where the sun had washed away all the color from the day, and as I walked along the perimeter, playing among the cactus flowers, something sharp stung my finger. I shouted, I screamed, I cried at the top of my lungs.

Nurses left the wounded soldiers and came running to take care of my sting. It was just a cactus, but I was duly impressed that they were so eager to help me.

We drove back home in the ambulance, and my father rushed down the stairs to open the door for us. He was not the least bit interested in any of the sights I had seen. His only interest was in my bandaged hand, and he questioned me about my injury.

"Dani," he repeated over and over. "You're sure you're okay? You're sure the finger doesn't hurt too much? You don't need to see a doctor? We'll watch over it to make sure it doesn't swell up or get more painful. Dani, are you okay?"

My father gave me so much to live up to. After the Munich Massacre, I often felt like I had let him down, had let the country down. I needed to rebuild my sense of self. I needed to find a way to justify my having lived.

At first I thought it would be fencing. Fencing became my independence as well as my way of emulating my father. I learned very young that life without fencing might not be life at all.

CHAPTER 5

Winning the Title/Winning the Girl

"When memory comes, knowledge comes too, little by little... knowledge and memory are one in the same thing."

Saul Friedlander, ***When Memory Comes***

Dan at age 19

Israeli team, 1969. Valdemar, his wife, Uri, Dan, Yoram, and Miki

When I was growing up, the fencing community in Israel was divided into two factions, the Ha Poel, centered in the Haifa area, and the Maccabi, whose offices were in Tel Aviv. My father, who was also my principle coach, was a member of the Maccabi group.

By my twelfth birthday, the two factions had split over some basic philosophical differences, and my father became frustrated with the political pollution of the sport. Despite the fact that fencing had been at the core of his life since his own childhood, he felt compelled to quit. He withdrew his membership from the Maccabis, and he put his swords away for good.

Not only did Abba stop competing and training himself, he suddenly stopped coaching me; then he went a step further and ordered me to hang up my swords next to his. All of a sudden, after six years of training, of breathing, eating, exuding fencing in my every day life, I found myself adrift. I had no place to fence, no coach. I needed a substitute sport, some other activity that would absorb my time; I was accustomed to the way fencing provided for my social life and enabled me to maintain my self-discipline and perseverance. I decided to give basketball a try.

Even then I knew that Basketball was a curious choice. I am not really a team player, I'm too individualistic, too solitary. So I tried swimming, which required overcoming my fear of water and learning to swim only after my father dropped me in the deep end of the neighborhood pool. I certainly was a strong swimmer and could swim for hours every day to remain in shape, but still I chose basketball as my new competition sport, and I played on a local team for four years.

Then, one bright spring day just before my 16th birthday, walking down the street, I was startled to hear my name called. "Dan Alon. I know you!"

I stopped, surprised, and though it took a moment, I did recognize him. He was David, a fencer and an official at a small club in Tel Aviv. I could not, however, fathom why he would want to speak to me.

"Danny, don't you remember me? I know you. I have often seen you fence."

I just stood there kind of stupidly staring, incredulous. "You were only twelve," David continued. "And you were very good. I remember that your father was coaching you – he, too, was a great fencer."

I was happy to launch into a recounting of the events that had led to Meir's retirement. "I miss fencing," I finally blurted. "I would like to fence again. But I have nowhere to go and no coach!"

"You should fence!" Encouraged David. "Come to my club, and I will see that you are coached. There's a Junior National Championship coming up in two months. You could win. I'll help you to prepare!"

Of course I could make no promise until I had been able to talk with my parents, so I vowed to let David know my answer as soon as I could. We bid one another good day and went our separate ways.

I could hardly contain myself. I felt my hand flex, imagining the sword's weight. My feet skittered, so that people passing probably thought me a dancer. Before I knew it, I had floated home, and only when I was nearly there did I realize how much I feared that they might deny me.

I knew that my parents would not be happy to hear this. My father was still bitter about the breakdown between the Israeli clubs, and my mother would worry about the strain the very discussion, let alone a return to the sport, would place on the family. But fencing was imbedded in my heart, so I decided I must not fail. I told myself to just keep talking stubbornly until they relented. I hadn't known till that moment how very much I missed fencing, how hungry I was for that Junior National Championship.

I entered the house and blurted my intentions. The more I talked, the more my mother shook her head; I reasoned, mother interrupted; I demanded, and Ima scolded. Blanka Alon would listen to no pleading, no cajoling, no arguing. She seemed hysterical to me, and her opposition felt utterly insane. She would allow no fencing in her home. It caused too much unhappiness, and she was in no mood to have her live disrupted by anything as insignificant as a sport.

My father just listened. His face was blank, but I half expected that he might jump in, take my side, and attempt to influence his wife on my behalf. After all, he had spent the better part of his life fencing; I felt he must have an inherent desire to pass the fencing tradition on to his older son. But he said nothing. A little later, I drew him out to the balcony, so that I could calmly present my case one more time. "I'm a good fencer, Abba," I pleaded. "Maybe I'm even better than good. And I'm not the kind of basketball player who will ever be invited to play on a world-class team. If I have any hope of making it to the Olympics – and, Abba, we have always wanted to go to the Olympics! – it has to be with an individual sport, and that has to be fencing. Fencing is my true sport. I inherited it from you. I have your gift, your drive, your dream." Papa looked deeply into my eyes, and then I knew I was home free.

Father took the argument to mother. At first, she remained obdurate, angry. But Abba continued to make our case, and I continued to dispute her opposition. In the end, our persistence won, but only after Ima had extracted an oath: I had to promise that I would train solely for the Junior Nationals. If I won the trophy, Mother would relinquish all opposition and allow me to return to fencing permanently. However, if I lost, even if I came in second, I was obliged to quit, to forget fencing forever. I agreed, and she relented. The next day I reported to David's club.

Thereafter, I went every day to that club and fenced. Soon, my father could not restrain himself. He would rush home to train with me. We would rearrange the furniture in the flat and spar right there in our living room. My mother rolled her eyes at the mess of fencing clothing and equipment scattered about the battered space, at the family belongings carelessly draped over the backs of displaced furniture, at the electric sound of embattled swords and scurrying feet. But she didn't make trouble; she knew we were in our element. And she knew I would keep my word.

My fencing visibly improved immediately, and Abba's renewed vigor for the sport was palpable. Fencing was clearly our life force, and we drove ourselves to new heights with each passing week. When the Junior National Championship date arrived, I was prepared. The meet was very near Tel Aviv, at the athletic center in Ramat Gan, and fencers came from all over the country to compete. It was like a homecoming for both of us. Father was delighted to be back among his friends – most of the coaches present were Hungarian fencers whose companionship he had missed since quitting the sport. For me, the highly competitive atmosphere was absolutely exhilarating.

Since this was the first time I had competed since I was 12, I was a complete surprise to the assembled fencers. Fencing in the classic French style, I had learned some technical tricks from Abba that enabled me to hit my opponents in ways they were not expecting. I was unusual and unusually proficient, so I easily won that Junior National Championship.

All around Israel, my victory was hailed under the banner headline, "Dan Alon, Fencer, Born With a Sword in His Hand." This was a Dan Alon no one had known before. My school friends, my teachers and coaches in school, all my most casual acquaintances were thrilled and treated me like a celebrity.

So, at 16, I had won a significant title; but more importantly, I had re-claimed my right to pursue my true passion. Even my mother allowed herself to smile, agreeing that I probably did have a future in fencing, that it would be a pity to give it up. "God gave you this talent," she allowed. "You must take care of it and make it grow."

While fencing was my focal point, I must admit that I was also just beginning to realize that perhaps there was more to life. During the Junior Nationals, I became friends with a group who introduced me to a vital piece of my country's history. And through them I met a girl who would be the first great love of my life.

Some of the best fencers in Israel came to the Junior Nationals in Ramat Gan from Degania, a kibbutz south of Lake Kineret near the Sea of Galilee. The fencers from Degania and I were naturally drawn to one another. Like most competitive athletes in individual sports, we recognized our common commitment to the sport and bonded through our mutual ardor.

I had never met any kibbutzim, the people who lived in the collectives. So the people of Degania fascinated me from the beginning. I had, of course, heard stories, read accounts of the simple, Spartan life on a kibbutz, but I grew up in the city, and I never imagined their kind of existence, one that was always difficult but always plain, uncomplicated and unadorned by consumerism.

By discovering Degania I discovered the heart of my country, and I found my own heart as well.

I knew that on a kibbutz people lived communally, sharing everything, laboring willingly for the good of the group, for the needs of the whole. I had learned that their social lives, their personal lives, their entire beings were centered in this all-encompassing kinship, and none of them ever needed to fear facing the world alone.

By contrast, my Tel Aviv world of the 1960's was very hectic. I was caught up in a continual social whirl, going to parties, interacting with youngsters who imitated the look of teenagers depicted in American films, listening to American rock'n'roll, dressing in American blue jeans and smoking American cigarettes. I could be a rebel with or without a cause, and I jealously guarded my uniqueness. My knowledge of American culture and my rabid individualism both bedazzled the young kibbutzniks. My cosmopolitan air quickly entranced them, just as I was enamored by their innate, irresistible idealism.

The Degania manager invited me and my teammates from Tel Aviv to spend the weekend on the kibbutz, a visit that would be highlighted by a one-on-one competition between the two teams. It would be a chance for the townies and the country boys to experience one another in a more relaxed setting, the manager suggested, a gift for both sides.

A chartered bus picked us up from our city school on Friday afternoon and dropped us at the Degania gate. We then entered a sequestered world.

Degania was perhaps the closest the modern world has come to achieving a utopia. Established in 1909 by a group of displaced Eastern European Jews, the settlement blended socialism and Zionism and created a collective – a kibbutz – where survival in the harsh, unwelcoming world of the desert could be affected through the principals of mutual dependency and social justice. Its founders called the kibbutz Degania, from the Hebrew word for "grain" in hopes that in its formation they might affect the seed of survival for their beleaguered people.

At first glance, life on the kibbutz was a continuation of the life my teammates and I brought from our city world. The bus dropped us in a common hall where we all broke bread together and immediately turned our attentions to the competition.

****

The moment the competition began, it was clear that Degania was a rarified world. The entire population of the collective – some 500 people – showed up to cheer for their fencers. Each time any Degania fencer registered a hit, the hall erupted in explosive joy, the kind rarely evident in the subdued world of fencing. But their excitement was not reserved for the home team. This huge, extended family took pleasure in the sport itself, and they were quick to show their appreciation for every accomplishment scored by either team.

Early on, I emerged the clear winner, and the crowd loved me. Before the tournament was over, I could feel their admiration, and I began to watch with wonder as they watched me with adoration. In the crowd, one face awed me the most, and soon that face became the only face I really saw at all. I promised myself that once the bout was over I would introduce myself and match a name to the face, but the girl to whom it belonged disappeared as though she had never been there.

The younger kibbutzniks besieged me for autographs, and many of the girls fawned over me, hoping to win my affection. But I was oblivious. She was not there, and I wanted to meet only her. I had no idea who she was. She was the most beautiful girl I had ever seen in my life! She had long, long blonde hair and eyes that were as green as the Jordan River. We did make eye contact once when I caught her watching, and my heart beat out of my chest.

At 16, I was in many ways a naïve child, having been a bit sequestered from interaction with the opposite sex. My life was immersed in my sport, and I had had little preparation for the secular world that included socializing with the other gender. My elementary education happened in a Jewish Day School, and my classmates were all boys; in high school, while I was good at pretending to be James Dean, I had no real experience with girls. I had always enjoyed a full social life with school parties and fencing events where girls and boys interacted in groups. But I had had no experience with pairing off, and I probably would have remained that way for some to come, except for Her.

When the fencing was over, the kibbutz threw a party to celebrate. This group, my new, albeit ersatz, family, seemed delighted to celebrate every small joy they experienced. And even though their team did not emerge victorious, they had derived pure pleasure from the engagement. So they threw a party.

Of course I went to the party, and she was there. But she had no interest in me whatsoever.

At first my Degania friends teased me. "Why would she want to meet you? Who are you after all? She is the most beautiful girl in the Jordan Valley; what makes you think she could be interested in you?" But I insisted, and my friends finally relented and introduced me.

That was the first time I ever felt a connection to a girl. Remembering her still makes me feel those same feelings – excited to know her, scared, nervous and shy, hoping she'd like me, but terrified. It was beautiful. And confusing. But beautiful.

When I returned to Tel Aviv, I received dozens of love notes from the girls on the kibbutz. But from my green-eyed Beatrice, I got nothing. I couldn't just pick up the phone and call her then. Telephoning was not all that easy in the '60's in Israel in general, but it was particularly difficult to reach anyone on a kibbutz by telephone. So, desperate to stay in contact with the object of my affections, I wrote to one of my friends in Degania and asked for her surname so that I might write to her.

Once I had her address, I composed a short note, telling the girl I would like to hear from her, admitting to her that I could not stop thinking about her. She responded immediately, but she expressed no emotion. The letter was coolly removed, but I tried to remain unperturbed. By this time, I was definitely in love. My first love!

That year, the fencers from Degania and I spent many weekends together. The kibbutz hosted a competition, and both Haifa and Tel Aviv were the venues for still others. When the kibbutzim visited Tel Aviv, I could play the part of city sophisticate, teaching my country friends how to dance, showing each of the boys how to impress a girl, how to hold her when dancing. They had no idea how inexperienced I really was, and they invited me often to visit their commune.

Now the difference between life in the city and life on the kibbutz took on a very real dimension. After we began to write one another, once she agreed to let me visit her on the kibbutz, that girl and I were never able to be alone. Like all the unmarried women there, she lived in a girls' dormitory. When she was a child, she had lived in the gan, the children's quarters, with the rest of the children, and she was accustomed to the fact that she had a host of sisters and brothers who were not her blood. On the kibbutz she had not one Jewish mother but many, and there were watchful paternal eyes everywhere she went.

The group ate in a community dining hall, read and played games and relaxed in great common areas, and they convened in an auditorium. Until they married, young men and women were always surrounded by their peers and always in sync with others. So my love was not requited in any real way, but I was content nonetheless.

Whenever I went to the kibbutz, I knew that my girl would be nearby. We talked more and more often, and we began exchanging letters. She became very real, very attainable, but I had no car to go back and forth between my home and hers; besides, I was so busy with fencing that having a girlfriend who was somewhat inaccessible was actually very attractive. Eventually I learned that she was only 13, and while I was undeterred, I understood that our relationship would be confined to the long-distance epistolary romance we had so artfully established.

Fencing took up more and more of my life after I won my first Junior Nationals championship. Immediately following competition, I was chosen to represent my team at the Maccabiad. The Maccabiah, or Maccabi Games, are a kind of Israeli Olympics. Every four years, in Olympics-alternate years, Jewish athletes from around the world come to Ramat Gan to compete. It is a highly competitive invitational event, especially in fencing, as many of the world's top-ranked fencers have traditionally been Jewish.

I was shocked to be selected as a Maccabiah Games athlete. I was still quite young for a fencer and, in my own estimation, sorely unprepared for such a competition. But, as ever, with my father's help, I rose to the challenge. So my young green-eyed beauty became an increasingly secondary consideration.

****

Fencing is a sport that demands maturity and experience in the mastery of excellence. The youthful vigor required for success in other sports is only useful up to a point, and fencers continue to improve often well into their forties and even their fifties. Being in the Maccabi Games fencing as a teenager against the greatest fencers from around the world gave me both the asset of strength and the deficit of experience that paled in comparison to that of the doctors, lawyers, university professors and others who had spent more years than I had lived perfecting their moves, honing their psychological advantages, studying the intellectual judgment so critical to scoring the hits. But I trained, and I faced my first international meet with aplomb.

Fencing against American and Canadian fencers for the first time, using their electric judging system – something entirely new to European and Israeli fencers – was thrilling. Especially satisfying was a bout I fenced against Albert Axelrod, who was on five consecutive American Olympic fencing teams; the bronze medal he won in the '60 Olympics was one of only fencing medals ever won by Americans in that sport.

At the time of the '61 games, Axelrod was ranked #1 in American fencing, as he was four times in his career – he was number two nine times. What impressed me most at the time was that he always defeated his German opponents who were the toughest fencers in the world. To be pitted against such a famous, formidable foe at my very tender age was the opportunity of a lifetime.

I remember being awed by the man's agility and strength and done in by his superior strategizing. But I was not the least bit disappointed when Axelrod won – Axelrod won six Maccabi titles in his career – because I knew that my performance validated my Olympic Dream. I thought, if I can hold my own against Albert Axelrod, I will make it to the Olympics for sure.

The girl with the green eyes was still at Degania, and I continued to visit her and my friends there for a few more times. But her youth and my inexperience and our very productive separate lives kept us apart. Soon it was time for me to fulfill my military obligation to my country.

Just before I left for the army, I went to Degania one last time. I managed to get the object of my affections to join me for a solitary walk around the grounds. We talked quietly over the bleating of the goats, stood and watched a friendly tennis match and dodged the commuters bicycling back and forth between work and play. She promised to write but made no further declarations, and I took this as a reason to hope that when I returned things would be as they were.

But of course they weren't. After the military, I went to Germany, and when I went to see her in advance of my trip to Cologne, she was about to enlist for her military service. Later, I heard she was appointed Secretary of the Air Force! I know I never really had a chance with her after all. But she was the great love of my imagination, and when she was gone, I strengthened my resolve to pursue the real great love of my life, fencing.

Yahrzeit: Yom Kippur War

"It is incredible what political simpletons Jews are. They shut their eyes to one of the most elementary rules of life, that you must not 'meet halfway' those who do not want to meet you."

   *Ze'ev Jabotinsky, **The Iron Wall**, November 4, 1923*

"The minute you raise a flag on a sports event, you invite politics in!"

   Yarin Kimor, 2007

"The only way to prevent politics from overtaking the Olympics is to eliminate all the team sports. Concentrate on individual sports and the athletes who compete. The games then focus on the athletic achievement rather than on any national identity, and more athletes could compete at a far higher level with far greater stakes."

   Dan Alon, 2012

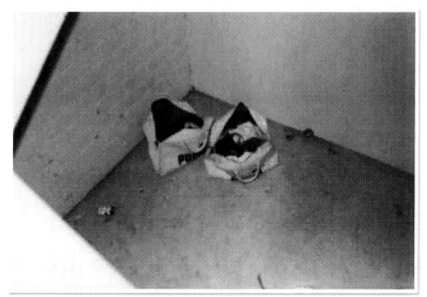

Bags discarded by the terrorists, most likely having contained weapons

Victims rooms after the massacre

It was somehow fitting that just a month after our first Yahrzeit, which was the first time we survivors had met since our shared torment, just as we had dedicated the headstones for our fallen brethren, our country was attacked on the highest, holiest day of our national and religious calendar.

We were caught unawares. It was a Tuesday afternoon, but because it was Yom Kippur, everything in the country had been shut down since the Kol Nidrei the night before. Like everyone else in the country, my family and I were in the synagogue, weakened by our fast, lulled by the cantor's music and the rabbi's sermon, feeling introspective. Then, at 2PM, an alert sounded, and it was a REAL alert. We were under attack from the air.

Everyone was instructed to go to their assigned shelters; my brother, my parents and I went to our home to prepare, and I got a phone call from my unit to report for active duty. We still had no clue what might be happening.

Outside was pandemonium. People were running out of the synagogues with tallis (prayer shawls) flopping, kippot (yarmulkes) flying every which way. Those who had driven got into their cars and drove quickly; the rest gathered their families together and ran. By 3PM, the fasting was over, and the country was mobilized.

I couldn't help thinking I was living through Munich again in a way. When we least expected it, we were attacked, and no outside forces came to our aid. We had thought we were done with war when we had won our stunning victory in the 6-Day War by quickly and efficiently vanquishing our enemies. But this time, the forces of eight nations – including two that are not even in the Middle East – invaded us together. On that Tuesday, October 6, we faced an offensive of troops that numbered more than the total NATO forces together, and NATO was not there to assist us.

One hundred eighty Israeli tanks faced one thousand, four hundred Syrian tanks, and our four hundred thirty-six fighters faced eighty thousand of the several million Egyptians Sadat had vowed to sacrifice along with their allies from Syria, Jordan, Lebanon, Saudi Arabia, Kuwait, Algeria and Morocco, all of whom were supported with weaponry – including guns, rockets, tanks and missiles – and intelligence from the Soviet Union. When the attack came, the United States, who had been our strongest, staunchest ally took a full week to respond to us, which essentially told Sadat he had their approval. We expected that; after all, Sadat had expelled many of his Soviet advisors in his effort to gain US support, and he had been successful.

We weren't so much surprised as caught at a weak moment. After all, Anwar Sadat had been railing about the territories we had won in the '67 War for years, and he had been threatening war at least since taking office in 1970, but he had not acted upon it. More than anything, the Arabs were motivated by their need to prove they could put us in our place. More than the territories they had lost in the '67 War, they wanted to regain their pride.

At the end of the Six-Day War, which took place from June 5-11, 1967, we had clearly triumphed. Our army was strong, we had consensus both at home and around the world. We were excited, and we had support from many sectors of the world; our achievement was exhilarating. We won the war with a minimum of time and money expended and, in the end it was a decisive victory. We decided the conditions of our treaties, created our own boundaries.

In three hours, the Israeli Air Force destroyed Egyptian, Syrian, Jordanian and Iraqi air force power. The infantry did the rest, and, after six days, the skies were clear for Israeli jets once more. The whole country came out to celebrate. Famous performers from Israel, from Europe, from the United States came to our bases to entertain us, and our planes flew overhead, proclaiming the safety of our very own air space.

The world took notice of Israel after the Six-Day War. The country's popularity grew for the next few years. World governments, press, power bases all took notice and admired us for our strength.

The Yom Kippur War, on the other hand, was very costly for us in almost every way. We fought for three weeks, having to push the Arabs way into Syria. Two thousand of our men were killed, and over eight thousand were wounded. Though our troops were technically victorious, we lost a great deal in the final analysis. Sadat's initial momentum gained a great deal of positive attention and brought him an expanded base of support from the global community. The treaty imposed on us required that we return territory won in the '67 War, and the Arabs were in many ways vindicated for their crushing defeat in the Six-Day War.

The cease-fire that ended the Yom Kippur War was imposed by the United Nations, and the UN brokered all the details of our tenuous peace. It wasn't until 1979 that a real treaty was signed, and by that time, we had lost much of the world's respect and had even earned a modicum of scorn; worse, we had lost our own self-esteem and our own consensus, a situation that weakens us still today.

Just like the Munich Massacre, the Yom Kippur War left us looking like victims. We lost our power by seeming to be weak, and the war seemed to have been precipitated at least in part by our own complacency. In Munich, Israel had trusted Germany to protect us – they had counted on German efficiency, on German attention to detail to ensure our safety, and that cost eleven men their lives. After the Six-Day War, the Israeli government trusted the US and the UN to be our allies, to come immediately to our aid; they were still complacent at the end of the war and left our fate in the hands of our very disappointing allies.

At the end of the Yom Kippur War, there was no absolute surrender by the aggressors; we allowed an attitude of conciliation, which further limits our ability to appear strong. In any conflict, the winner is the one who takes the upper hand, but just as we had in the aftermath of the massacre, we relinquished that upper hand by allowing others to stipulate the war-ending parameters.

During the standoff in Munich, Golda Meir, Moshe Dayan and the Mossad all asked that the Germans allow Israeli commandos rescue the athletes. The Germans were adamant that no Israeli military would take action on German soil. They were so uncompromising in their unwillingness to allow Israel to engage in protecting her own athletes, that they even went so far as to bar Zvi Zamir, the Mossad Chief, from interviewing the hostages or getting near the rooms where they were being held. Germany and the world allowed our athletes to be sacrificed and prevented any Jew from participating in any effort to fight back. Israeli paratroopers, at the ready to rescue the hostages, were prohibited entry to the country, and the hostages' well-being was held in the iron grip of a country bent on handling things themselves.

In the same way that the Germans had bungled the release and resolution of the standoff with Black September, the United Nations fumbled our safety after the Yom Kippur War. The perception of our weakness grew in the eyes of the Hezballah because no action was initiated to stop them in their continued quest to eradicate us from the earth. Even at the moment of our great terror, when a handful of Black September extremists held our team in its death grip, the Germans and the rest of the world held their breath and hoped rather than taking a decisive stand that might have saved the captive athletes. There is a continual problem at the Lebanese border, and no decisive action is taken by the world community to curtail it except to ask us to forfeit land we won in the war we fought to prove we can survive.

After the Yom Kippur War, I began to feel insecure in Israel. Of course, this was exacerbated by my experience in Munich, but Israel became a far more insecure place to live, to do business. I thought I would have to leave, to make my life elsewhere, but in the end, I couldn't leave, and I have changed my mind. There is only one place in the world for me, and that is in Israel. It's our land, the only piece of land that belongs to us in the universe. Everywhere else in the world the Jew is a guest, but here we are home. We are in our own place.

Munich will always be part of our national insecurity. It has changed the country the way it has changed me. When I was a child, the Israeli people were calmer, happier, more idealistic. They were hopeful, and they dreamed of creating a stable, peaceful Jewish state.

Today, the Israeli people are weary, fatigued from all the fighting, all the criticism we receive from around the world. It shouldn't matter, but it does. We know we have nowhere else to go, nowhere else where we are truly welcome, but the world expects us to move over and let a people dedicated to the proposition that we have no right to be here have power equal to or greater than ours. So, everywhere in Israel, people have become more aggressive, less polite than ever. You don't get such good service in restaurants, and you don't get as much friendliness and cooperation from your compatriots.

Israel needs peace. Real peace. But for peace, you need patience, cleverness, and imagination. We need shrewd, skillful, talented leadership in our parliament, on the economic advisory committees that counsel the legislators, and we need help with our public relations. At the moment, the Arabs are far better at currying public favor than we are, and that hurts us.

Just before the Six-Day War, there was a very popular song written by Naomi Shemer, called *Yerushalayim shel Zachav* – Golden Jerusalem – about the beauty of our beloved city and the triumph of having returned there. It was like an anthem that we sang to celebrate jubilantly in a single voice the night we celebrated our victory; it became unofficially our second national anthem.

There have not been such moments since then for us. And Munich solidified our sadness, leaving us in need of a new infusion of optimism. But I think peace is still a long way away.

I have a theory that Israel and the Middle East are not yet ready for peace in any meaningful way. The world is pressuring them to make a peace, at great cost to Israel, and it cannot possibly succeed at this time. The process is too large. Europe is the perfect paradigm. For hundreds of years, before WWII, Europe was at war with itself. It was 2,000 years in the making and is now a unified continent, a great world center, but the achievement was won at great cost.

I actually got this notion when I was fencing once in Scandinavia. I was in a café in Denmark, watching the world go by, conversing with my Danish friends, drinking coffee, looking over the water at Sweden. I commented to them how good it felt to see such neighbors, such good friends among the countries. One of my Danish friends remarked, "Do you realize that we fought the Swedes for 400 years to make this peace? We were at war for centuries. Do you expect to have peace so soon? How long has your country been in existence? Only since 1948! That's nothing. No time at all. Your country is too young for peace; it's just too soon."

He's still right. We are only in our sixty-fourth year. We Jews only returned to this land in any major way a hundred years ago. The process must be allowed to take its own time. The people in the Middle East must learn to accept the Jews back after their 2,000-year absence. Who knows how long that will take? But there needs to be more dialogue and longer dialogue. You can't push to make peace or to find a paper solution. To believe that makes us as naïve as the Germans were about themselves at Munich.

Wearing sky blue uniforms and being unarmed didn't make them peacekeepers in Germany. They tried to impose a false security in a place where none was truly in place. It was too fragile. It couldn't hold up.

You can't speed the process. There are no short cuts.

> Yerushalayim shel zahav
> Veshel nechoshet veshel or
> Halo lechol shirayich Ani kinor.

> *(translation)*
> *Oh, Jerusalem, of gold and light and bronze,*
> *I am the lute for all your songs.*

CHAPTER 7

Approaching Xanadu

"The goal of Olympism is to place sport at the service of the harmonious development of man, with a view to promoting a peaceful society concerned with the preservation of human dignity."

The Olympic charter – Principals of the Olympics #2

Raising of the Israeli flag, the day we arrived in Munich

My father's dream of being an Olympic contender passed on to me, and in 1971, I began to see myself making it a dream-come-true; I knew that I would qualify at long last for the 1972 Olympics. But it was the culmination of many years of rigorous and demanding training and preparation – and a good deal of entertaining fun as well. As the press so often reminded me, I was indeed born with a sword in hand, but becoming a world-class athlete in that sport was not merely a birthright; I had to earn that.

When I was very small, I would go with my father to his fencing club, and I was never just a casual observer. I was a very serious, very focused little boy; by then I had begun to expect perfection from myself in everything I took on, from my art to my athletics. I would watch my father, and by age 3, I could imitate his footwork, match his rhythms. When I reached age 6 or so, my father agreed to allow me to begin to study fencing, but I was not permitted to touch a weapon. I was to concentrate on my footwork, on the steps I needed to perfect in order to be a well-choreographed swordsman. Abba told me I would not even touch a sword until my feet were expert at what they needed to do.

For a six-year-old, training in footwork was exceedingly boring, but I stuck with it, forcing myself to practice daily, to watch closely when my father and his friends fenced, to copy the way their feet danced on a piste. I hated it, but I knew that my reward would be the sword I longed to hold.

After three years – during which time I thought of myself more as playing than training – my father allowed me to begin to fence. My fingers were still small, still too weak to hold a weapon correctly, so I fenced only with children. By the time I reached 11, I was ready for my first competition, and I fenced in the 16-and-under category.

There was a local jeweler who created the medals for our competitions, and I fell in love with the artwork he produced. I decided that I must have one of these custom-designed medals, and I practiced even harder, intent on winning for the sake of that piece of jewelry! It was a delicious victory when I won and got to wear that medal, but nothing compared with the feeling of pure joy I derived from the look of pride and pleasure in my father's eyes as I stood for the photographers who recorded my moment. I realized how very deeply my father believed in me, how very willing he was to transfer his Olympic dream to me, even though he had been our National Champion many times since 1948 and would never attend an Olympiad.

As I have already written, I was forced to stop fencing for a few years when I was 12, until my first coach David discovered me on the street in Tel Aviv. Within two months of our meeting, I was back in competition, my father was coaching me regularly, and I had begun to win. I fenced in Ramat Gan, in Haifa, all over Israel, and I knew I would be competing outside the country in no time. For three years I held the Junior National Title, and no one could wrest it from me. Then, when I was 16, I was chosen to represent Israel in the international Maccabiah Games of 1961.

The year I was 16, I also found a new mentor, a professional coach who had been a world-class fencer in Hungary. My father was an excellent coach, but a father-son relationship is no good in competition; there is too much room for disagreement, for discord. So my father took me to his friend Alfred Noble, and it was Alfred Noble who became my coach. I began to specialize somewhat in the saber; up until then, I had competed equally on all three blades – the epee, the foil and the saber, which was my father's weapon of choice – and had even won championships in all three events. I continued, in fact, to work on my foil fencing with a Romanian coach and later, in Germany, with an Italian who improved my foil fencing immeasurably. But Noble was a saber fighter, and so he encouraged me to develop a specialty, which I did, with the saber.

I was ecstatic over the Maccabiad. It would be my first opportunity to fence among adults, as the Maccabiah Games are held every four years, in non-Olympic years, and bring together world class athletes from all over the US and Canada. I would be fencing with IOC Fencing equipment and rules, being judged electronically for the first time. This was a totally new system for me, one that had was accurate to a fault, with no space for human error. And, perhaps more importantly, I would be fencing for the first time against athletes who had competed internationally, especially one New Yorker named Albert Axelrod, who had already competed in Mexico City, Chicago and Rome and been a gold, bronze and silver winner. This was a huge moment for me; I felt then that I had arrived.

From then on, I spent my weekends training in earnest. At the club, I fenced with the locals, who were largely an academic group, intellectual weekend warriors. My best training partner was my brother Yoram, who was quickly approaching my own level of expertise and skill, and I was very lucky because as my training schedule intensified, Yoram was always with me, which meant that the competition trips would always be both fruitful and fun.

We were often in Paris, where I had a great relationship with an older woman, a fencing fan named Sylvie, who came to see me with gifts of food and wine every time I was in town. In Spring, 1971, Yoram and an Israeli fencer named Mickey Vardi and I were there for the DuVal competition, a huge inter-European fencing match, where we all hoped to be noticed as a preliminary to the Olympics, which were, by then, only four years away. I was already well known as a fencer in France, and this match was important enough that the Israeli embassy sent representatives to watch the competition, to encourage us and to applaud for us when we won. They even assigned a security person to our group, someone who was there just to make sure that at all times we were safe. Actually, at the time I was sure the security man was from the Israeli embassy, but after Munich I wondered if he were actually assigned by the French, who seemed more aware of potential dangers than either the Israeli or the Germans were in 1972. But in any case, during the DuVal, I finished number 20 out of 200 fencers, which was a huge success because I had needed to place well in order to clear my path toward qualifying for the Olympics.

We stayed in Paris for ten days; my brother and Vardi didn't even finish the first round, so they were out of the competition early and disqualified for the Olympics, and after a couple days, Vardi disappeared. He just vanished into thin air, and we didn't have a clue where he was. But we were too busy to worry about it. Besides my fencing, we were exploring the city of Light with the lovely Sylvie. We were in a top-flight hotel, near L'Opera in the Pigalle area where all the best nightclubs were, and we ate in the finest restaurants. When our stipends from the Israeli Sports

Federation were inadequate to pay for our fun, Sylvie took care of us.

The very last night, with only $60 between us, we decided we had to go out and celebrate.

Yossi, our friend from the embassy, was skeptical. "Dani, you don't have nearly enough money to do anything extravagant. I think we need to stay in and –"

"You're right, Yossi," I laughed. "We are nearly broke. So let's take a taxi!"

"Where are we going?" Yoram asked with some trepidation.

"The Lido," I replied with enthusiasm.

"But, Dani, we agreed that we were not going to let Sylvie pay for another night of entertainment. It's too much."

"You're right, Yoram. I have an idea. We'll sit at the bar and watch the show from there. We will leave our coats in the hotel so we won't have to pay for them, and we'll share a single bottle of champagne."

Poor Yoram needed to go to the bathroom, but we wouldn't let him go because the bathroom cost money. We had a fabulous time, and we still had money left, which we used to get to the airport in the morning. Unfortunately, when we arrived at the airport, the ride cost twice what we had. We couldn't do anything but give the driver everything. He was still yelling at us when we walked into the terminal, but Vardi never showed up.

The adventure had not ended either. Our suitcases were overweight, and we had no money to pay for them. Luckily, we found some strangers who had little luggage, and they agreed to take some of our baggage.

I returned to Israel knowing my hard work was paying off and feeling like I led a charmed life. Vardi, on the other hand, never returned to Israel. We learned later that he had met a blonde woman, had fallen in love and had remained in France. I don't think it phased me in the slightest -- what I knew then was that I was one step closer to my Olympic dream.

We competed throughout Europe. One trip took us by train through Germany and Scandinavia; other trips took us to Switzerland, where we competed in Bern, Geneva and Zurich, Belgium and the Netherlands.

One of our trips was prolonged by the fact that my father had his first heart attack in Frankfort, and he had to remain in the hospital there for three months. So Yoram and I stayed in German and traveled to all the competitions in Europe, always returning to Germany to visit with Father after the rest of our team returned to Israel.

The most significant thing about that particular period was that it was the first time that Israel had a full team competing in Europe, and we were very successful. We beat the Swiss National team and the Belgian National Team. We scored well in Holland and continued on to Denmark, where we made our mark again. In each country, in addition to our matches, we engaged in our usual explorations of the social scenes in our host countries.

In Amsterdam, my brother and I shared a hotel room. Because he was still very young and not so keen on nightlife, I spent evenings alone, seeking out the fun places to play by night. One evening, I returned to the hotel very late to find the place locked up tight, and I didn't have a key. I had arrived in a taxi and didn't know exactly what to do; the taxi driver was concerned, so he stayed right there with me while I figured it out. There was no way in. I was pretty sure where the window to my room was, so I shouted again and again from the middle of the street. "Yoram. Yoram. Wake up!!" I kept shouting for a very long time. Finally, just as I was beginning to think I would be sleeping in the street, I saw his face peeking out from the room window. I thought for sure he'd come down right away and let me in, but at least ten or fifteen minutes went by before there was another sign of him. I kept shouting, and the cab driver, who had a huge, booming voice, shouted with me. "Yoram. What are you doing? I'm here, and I need to come in!" Finally, Yoram came to the door.

"I didn't know who would call my name from the street," he said. "I thought I was dreaming."

In Denmark, we shared our room with Mickey Vardi. The three of us went out together, and I was usually the one who scored well with the women. But one night, Mickey invited me to go with him to the bar, and I preferred to go back to sleep for the big competition in the morning. I told him I'd stay in, but after a couple hours, I went out to look for him.

There he was in the hotel bar with a beautiful blonde Danish woman, and I was jealous. I decided to join them, and at midnight, I realized one of us would have to take her to her room Neither of us was willing to give in to the other, and each waited for the other to say he was tired and going to bed. Finally, we asked if we could both escort her home. She laughed.

"You're really nice Israelis," she said. "But I must insist you make a choice between yourselves which will take me home."

We both said we would return to our room and rest for competition, and she agreed to take herself home. But I was young and arrogant and not ethical. While Mickey was paying the bill, I took her to her room and didn't see Vardi till the next day. He would not speak to me.

In the end, I got my just desserts. We lost our competition against Denmark, and I knew it was because of my bad behavior. Mickey reported me to the Israeli Fencing Committee, and I was punished. From then on, when we traveled in Sweden and Finland, I was confined to my room and never allowed to leave.

I didn't see Stockholm, but we fenced well and won our match against Sweden.

In Finland, my house arrest was relaxed. It was freezing in Helsinki – couldn't have been warmer than 20 C – but I was at my best. Against a very strong Finnish team, we performed very well, and I won the title for Israel.

I couldn't help noticing that there were two Finnish girls who couldn't take their eyes off me. After the competition, they invited me to go to the disco with them, and I told them I would have to get permission from the Head of the Delegation. It was very embarrassing, but he allowed me to go. I called Vardi – I figured this would be a chance to make up for some of my bad behavior toward him – and invited him to celebrate. We left my brother in the hotel and went to the disco till 6 a.m. In order to get to our flight in time, we were supposed to be leave for the airport at 7. Of course, my brother was furious when I returned at the last possible moment and caused us to have a crazy ride from the hotel to the airport. But we made it. We flew from Helsinki to Sweden and then took a train to Germany. I slept for twenty-four hours straight!

The last year before the Olympics was a really special year. After the Spring of '71, when I was 20th out of 200, which meant that I was among the twenty best fencers in all of Europe, and I thought I would automatically qualify for the Olympics, but that was not the case. I needed one more competition in Europe to make the team, and that was scheduled in April, 1972. I knew that if I failed there, I would not go to Munich.

At the time, I had been fencing in meets using all three weapons, and I was the only person in my country ever to be National Champion in epee, foil and saber. Now, heading into the final stretch before the Olympics, my coaches decided that I should concentrate on the Foil, even though I was a splendid saber competitor. My father was not altogether happy about this, as he, of course, was a saber fencer.

No matter, I fenced every day and went to every competition I could manage to get into my schedule that year. I easily won the Israeli National Championship and all kinds of lesser trophies, and in January 1972, I won the Yehuda Prize, another National honor.

Then, in April of '72 my team and I traveled to a small area called Offenbach, near Frankfurt for some friendly competition between the local team and our own. The German team put us up in a lovely area outside the city, surrounded by quiet woods, and we all enjoyed both the fencing and the socializing with one another. Everyone enjoyed the local apple wine!

From there, I went to what would be, for me, a hugely important competition. The Coronation Cup in London is a highly, prestigious, popular competition, and that year there where 150 fencers from all over Europe competing, as was I, in order to finalize their eligibility for the Olympic Games.

I was very nervous and also extremely excited. Physically, I was in great shape, but mentally, I was in no condition to compete. So I asked the Israeli federation to send me to London with a psychologist instead of a coach. And in this I lucked out.

One of the people who traveled and fenced with our team was a doctor of psychology, a prominent practitioner in the field. I asked him to escort me to the Coronation Cup competition in London, and, with the approval of the federation and my coaches, we flew from Frankfurt to London on a Friday morning for a

Saturday morning meet. My German friends and teammates all came to the airport to wish me much luck and success.

I was so hyper-excited that I hadn't slept in a few nights, but the moment we boarded the airplane, the doctor began to talk. Amazingly, he opened conversation about everything BUT fencing. We talked about politics, about music, about art, about girls. When we arrived in London, we went to the British Museum, where we stayed till evening, and I had no time to think about fencing or to do anything to prepare for the meet. The doctor explained what he knew about art and archeology, which was considerable, and I was fascinated. I admit I didn't even think about the Coronation Cup – this doctor was so intelligent and so pleasant to be with, I was completely absorbed in the museum and our conversation.

After we got back to our rooms, I fell asleep immediately, and the next morning, we went to the fencing hall for the competition. I was calmer than I had been in years and had nearly forgotten what I was there to do. We continued our talking on our way to the hall, and we were still talking when we reached the venue.

I knew that I needed to reach the quarterfinals in this competition, which meant I must be among the top 24 fencers. It seemed a difficult point to reach because it was apparent that these 150 fencers were among the best in all Europe. I knew I could do it; I just needed to be psychologically strong.

Five minutes before the meet was to begin, my friend the doctor took me aside and, for the first time, he talked to me about fencing. "Look, Dani," he said. "Here we are in London, where Shakespeare was when he wrote his play *Hamlet*. Hamlet asked the question, 'To be or not to be?' That is for you a very critical point. If you win this competition, you are in the Olympics. If you lose, you are out. It's time to BE.'"

All over Israel, in Germany, wherever I had friends, colleagues, fellow fencers and supporters, people were awaiting the results. And at the end of the day, I was exhilarated to let them know that I had made the top twelve! At that point, nothing more mattered. I had attained my goal for the meet. My psychologist and I were so happy, we danced and sang and hugged and kissed one another, but then I couldn't reach anyone back home. Of course, in those days, no one had mobile phones, and long-distance telephoning was imperfect at best. So, after all that, I had to wait to tell everyone until we returned to Germany. I would have been terribly deflated, but I was so high on the achievement that I was able to sustain the mood until we reached Frankfurt, where the team was assembled, awaiting our arrival.

My heart sank when we got there and found they were not in the hotel. For a moment I thought I would burst, but the doctor suggested we go to the pub and wait for them there. And, of course, when we opened the door to the pub, there they all were drinking apple wine, anxiously expecting some news.

"Well, Dani," asked my brother, speaking for the group. "Well?"

"Very well, dear Yoram. I DID IT!!!! I have made it into the Olympic Games in Munich!!!"

That night, we celebrated like there was no tomorrow. Everyone in the town, even strangers, celebrated with us, and we drank more apple wine than I ever thought I could hold. My brother got so drunk he bought a big bunch of flowers and gave everyone a single flower as he sang to them in Hebrew. We had a great evening.

I think, however, that the best part of my night was reaching my father on the phone. I could hear him sob as I told him that his dream had come true for me. "I'm going to the Olympics, Abba," I announced proudly. And I could feel his joy vibrate right through the telephone.

We flew back to Israel, and every newspaper in the country ran a story the next day about me, my father, and our Olympic dream. The local television station did a ten-minute documentary about me for prime time broadcast, and the cameras followed me through a day in my life, recording me at home, at my office, at my fencing club. What I loved most of all about that film, a copy of which I still cherish, was that they interviewed my father and featured him in the program. So I have a living memento, my father speaking to these interviewers about fencing and about me. It was a glorious feeling.

Two weeks after I qualified, one of the leading Israeli newspapers ran a poll asking that people cast votes designating who, in their eyes, were the best athletes in the country. The poll asked the readers to name athletes from all sports and athletic activities, and I was named the best fencer and an athlete among the very best in the country! The newspaper awarded me a trophy with the poll results on it.

By this time, I was fencing every evening and every day, but three months before the Olympics, they arranged for me to practice at a place called the Wingate Institute, the Israeli sports academy, where the normally train people for careers in physical education, fitness training, gymnastics coaching, etc. Wingate offers athletes from all sports complete immersion in the work and is made available to Olympic athletes in advance of the games; the federation houses the athletes at the institute, which provides them the opportunity to bond and become a truly united delegation.

That is where I first met the other athletes who would be with me at Munich, and we all worked very hard, increasing our training by adding swimming and running and weight training to our routines. I became very good friends with the wrestlers and weight lifters, the ones I would soon lose, in those days at the Wingate. The staff there fed us well, the doctors monitored our health, and everyone worked overtime to make sure we were all well cared for, but it was still exhausting work. However, we all knew how important it was, and we kept one another going.

Mark Slavin, the Greco-Roman wrestler, was just a kid then – he had just turned 18 in January – but he had emigrated from the old Soviet Union, and he showed me the true, Russian way to use a sauna. He poured vodka and beer over the stones, and though it made me a bit dizzy, I couldn't get enough of it. I showed everyone what Mark had taught me, and the sauna was the hit of our Wingate stay.

I think of Mark whenever I hear the very word sauna.

CHAPTER 8

Collision of Dreams

"With whom would the just not sit

To help the cause of justice?

If you could change the world at last,

What would be beneath you?

Who are you?

Sink in the dirt,

Embrace the Slaughterer,

But change the world: the world needs you!"

> Bertholt Brecht

Munich airport before returning to Tel Aviv. Dan Alon second from right.

A truism I find difficult to justify is that to the Palestinians the Munich Massacre was justifiable violence, a necessary part of their process of gaining world recognition. The American Civil Rights activist Malcolm X theorized that a people should achieve equality "by whatever means necessary," and Bertholt Brecht would have applauded such treachery in theory. But neither Brecht nor Malcolm X ever perpetrated such a horror; both understood that in the real world, violence only breeds more violence, and pain only extracts more pain. However, the Palestinians in particular and terrorists in general see only the instant gratification of getting their way, of diverting all eyes from all other global events to themselves, and they content themselves with the notion that they will have eternal peace once they have sacrificed themselves – along with untold others – and gone to Heaven.

After the 1948 War, Israel's borders were redefined. The Egyptian border was restored to its pre-war line, except that part of the Gaza Strip that Egypt continued to control. The Lebanese border was reestablished where it was before the war, as was the border with Syria. Jordan kept Judea and Sumeria, traditionally named the West Bank, and Jordan held control over the Old City of Jerusalem. Many Palestinians went into exile, and so began the root cause of the Munich Massacre: the Palestinian refugee problem.

When the Palestinians left Israel, they left in a panic. Rumors had been spread that the Jews were about to massacre the whole Palestinian population, that they would plow the Palestinians into the ground, and the people believed the rumor. In the chaos that ensued, most of the nearly 500,000 displaced Palestinians went to Syria, some to Jordan, Egypt and to Lebanon. They had been encouraged, even coaxed, by their fellow Muslims to leave Israel, and they were further advised to stay out of Israel. But this left them virtually homeless. The Israelis extended an invitation for 100,000 Palestinians to return, but the offer was rejected.

In the Arab countries, the Palestinians found work or they starved, receiving no help from Islamic governments. After the 1967 War, the Arab states began to harden toward the Palestinians. Those people who had been living in territory taken from Syria, Lebanon and Jordan, who stayed within the new Israel, found that the Israeli government assumed responsibility for their placement, helped them seek employment, and offered them health care and other benefits, whether they were working or not. The other governments responded with heightened wariness and suspicion, which only added insult to the injury of the displacement suffered by the Palestinians. The United Nations offered remuneration to countries who would shelter the refugees, give them citizenship and services, but none of the Arab countries would take them in.

When I traveled around after the war, I could see the signs of trouble everywhere. Thanks to the expansion of our borders, hundreds of thousands more Palestinians were driven into refugee camps within our country because they were not welcome in Syria, Jordan, or Lebanon. Yasser Arafat got busy expanding his Fatah, the largest party in the Palestine Liberation Organization, the consortium of Palestinian nationalist liberation groups he founded. He established satellites in Syria, Jordan and Lebanon, and he raised troops and money, waging his own war on the Jewish foe at home and all over the world.

There was no mistaking what was on the horizon. The Arab leaders didn't approve of the PLO activities. How could they? They understood what Israel knows, that the PLO has but one purpose, and that is to establish a Palestinian State and oust the Jews from the land entirely. They will then likely wage war against the other Arab states, seeking vengeance for the summary way they were shunned. The Palestinians could easily have established a state in any Arab nation and called it their own, and it would have been as meaningful as the land they want to reclaim from Israel.

King Hussein of Jordan was the first Arab leader to openly show his power in an effort to curtail the activities of the Fatah and the Popular Front for the Liberation of Palestine (PLFP), both factions of the PLO, operating in his country. There, the refugees had their lives entirely transformed, as the king prohibited El Fatah, PFLP, and all armed forces of the Palestinian resistance. He did not like looking bad in the press, and the international media had given him a very hard time for not acting decisively. King Hussein didn't like anything that threatened his power either, and he could see the PLO groups might threaten his sovereignty.

A series of confrontations between Hussein and the Fattah ensued. On September 17, 1970, Hussein launched an all-out attack on the Palestinian guerrillas that left at least 4,000 fedeyeen – warriors – dead. The Palestinians named the event Black September and blamed the Jews for all of it.

The Palestinians tried to move their operations to Syria, but their activities there were scrutinized, and the worst was that the Syrian Bedouins couldn't get along with the Palestinians. Syria was not a good placement for them. The moved on to Lebanon, and that turned out to be a viable alternative.

In Lebanon, the government allowed the PLO to control their own refugee camps and to set up training bases for anti-Israel operations. The refugees formed a new faction of the PLO, called Black September, devoted, from the beginning, to meting out vengeance on those who had killed and injured the 4,000, including their leader Abu Ali Ayad. Today, Black September operates all over the world, and they function in splintered, disparate clusters so they are very difficult to track. These are the terrorists who make me the most uneasy.

Black September fighters are divas. They will do anything for attention. They like to think they are warriors, that because they are willing to die for a victory, they are heroic. They liken themselves to the Japanese Kamikaze. But they have no honor. The Kamikaze attacked warplanes and aircraft carriers; they targeted armed foes. Black September, like other terrorists, target weak, unprotected civilians. They look for old people, for children, for the helpless, and then they sneak around planting bombs and sniping from hidden, protected citadels.

Munich was one in a series of attacks they perpetrated in the 1970's and probably the least amateurish. In 1971, Black September introduced itself by assassinating the Jordanian Prime Minister, and then in December of that year, they attempted the assassination of King Hussein and his upper level advisors. In early May, 1972, Black September attempted to hijack a Sabena airline from Israel as it was about to land in Vienna. Israeli commandos managed to thwart the laughable, amateurish plot; they swiftly took control of the plane and took the terrorists into custody. It was a terrible embarrassment to the entire PLO and led to a terrible massacre at the end of the month.

On May 30, three armed members of the Japanese Red Army, trained by and acting on behalf of Black September and the PFLP in Lebanon, killed 26 people in Lod International Airport and injured 80 more. Among the dead were seventeen Christian pilgrims returning to Puerto Rico, one Canadian, and eight Israelis, including the brother of Ephraim Katzir, our soon-to-be President. When it was all over, it became clear that the operation was intended to be much larger, a suicide mission that should have included international participants – Irish and Japanese recruits – but constituted a victory for the terrorists in that it provided Black September with the attention they craved. They got a huge amount of press and were in the limelight for some time; the entire terror community was impressed with their work.

About eight to nine months before the Olympics, Andrei Spitzer was brought in by the Israeli Olympic Committee to be our coach. He and Ankie had a studio in one of the new border towns on the Lebanese border, a town called Biranit, in the shadow of Camp Biranit, where the Israeli military patrols the border and protects the country from the Hezbollah, religious extremists whose name means literally "God's army." It was to that studio that the Committee sent Yehuda and me to train when we were selected to represent Israel at the Olympics.

Training in Biranit was a good experience. We could be fencers twenty-four hours a day, and Andrei, Yehuda and I were Israeli Three Musketeers, always together, inseparable companions, always ready to brandish our swords. We became very close, like brothers.

While we were in Biranit, Hezbollah were the omnipresent. The armed militia of Lebanon, their raids on our borders ever imminent, we knew the Hezbollah and what to expect from them. They have always been a consistent threat, attacking when attacked, operating like an army. They are very different from the various factions of the PLO, who live at the fringes of our frontiers nibbling at our lines, attacking our buses; the PLO continually fought us and fought one another as well as the Lebanese government. We trusted the Hezbollah, in a way, because they were a known quantity, a paramilitary force that in Biranit was never far from our consciousness but never really a threat.

Every day in Biranit, we practiced, rehearsing for our appearance at the Olympic Games. We brandished our weapons, perfected our strategies for outwitting our opponents. We exercised our muscles to make them ever stronger, ever more resilient. At night we frequented the local pubs and mingled with the soldiers and the locals, who told us all about their community.

One day I heard something I found interesting at the time but chilling after Munich. Just on the other side of the border, minutes away from us, on the Lebanese side, a group of Black September was training for something. We thought they might even have an Olympic team of some kind because they were so diligent in their training, but then we learned that they had been denied the right to send a delegation to Munich because they were not a sovereign country. We weren't sure what they were doing, but they were definitely training.

All the time we were there, Black September was aggressively training, brandishing their weapons, perfecting their strategies for outwitting their opponents, preparing for their appearance at the Olympic Games. They exercised their muscles to make them ever stronger, ever more resilient.

I wonder if they mingled with the Hezbollah. I wonder if they were aware of us.

CHAPTER 9

Living by the Sword: A Brief and Personal Look at Fencing and its History

"The whole art of fencing consists in just two things: to hit and not to be hit."

Molière, *Le Bourgeois Gentilhomme.*

Dan Alon at age 16

Then – The Deadly Game

"If we duel and you win, death for me. If we duel and I win, life for you."

Inigo Montoya, *The Princess Bride*

There are so many ways in which my destiny was intertwined with fencing. Of course, the emblem of the Israeli Defense Force, our national protectors, is a sword wrapped in an olive branch, which, if you consider it, has resonance for a fencer who uses his sword in peace. I think about my promise as an artist, and I am reminded that one of the most famous swordsmen in 16th C Florence was Michelangelo Buonarroti Simoni, the great painter of the Sistine Chapel in Rome and the sculptor of David. Michelangelo, in fact, is said to have been such a fan of swordsmanship that he volunteered to illustrate the definitive book on Italian swordplay by his close friend Camillo Agrippa. In London, my psychologist helped me to win my place in the Munich Olympics at the Coronation Cup by discussing *Hamlet* with me, and *Hamlet* was the first play ever to place a fencing duel at the center of its dramatic climax.

Fencing is a combination of dance and gymnastics; it requires chess-like strategies and brute strength, agility and stamina. It is the sport of kings, but it was once deadly combat, and it evolved from the military practices of ancient Egypt.

According to historians and anthropologists, the first swords appeared as weapons sometime between 1500 and 1100 BC, in what are now Crete and Britain. But even as they were being developed for use in battle, they were already being used for sport by the time they were adopted by the Egyptians of the Upper Kingdom during the 1190's BC. Sport was not, as it is today, a safe, entertaining match of wit and dash; it was, rather, a blood sport, a fight to the death performed for crowds who loved to watch opponents engage in mortal combat.

An engraving found on a temple built during the reign of Ramses III depicts a practice match of some sort. The swordsmen are wearing masks and ear padding, and their weapons are swathed in some kind of protective cloth. Judges holding feathered wands watch the session, and they are keeping score on a papyrus sheet. On the right of the engraving, there is a pile of severed penises, trophies taken from the enemy dead. An inscription reads, "On guard and see what my valiant hand can do." It would be a very long time before the victors' spoils ceased to be the lives of the vanquished.

Swords and sport displaying men's agility with them appear in most ancient culture. In Japan, China, Persia, Babylon and Rome, the sword was primarily, at least at first, for war, but from the very beginning it was a showpiece for the Greeks, Persians and Indians. Although the Greeks discredited swordsmanship, pointing out that in combat, it was nearly impossible to miss a foe, they encouraged athletes to wield swords for strength and agility training, as well as for exhibition. The Indians believed that the god Brahma taught priests and warriors how to use a sword. *The Mahabharata*, the world's longest epic, written by Sanskrit poet Vedavaysa in 3012 BC (or thereabouts), describes the swordsman as "ferocious and chivalrous," his action "quick and light." In ancient Persian texts, agility with a sword was considered to be as basic as breathing, and the Egyptians clearly used sword fighting for entertainment as well as for military purposes; a wall painting from around 1200 BC depicts two men fencing with saber-like swords. Their forearms are wrapped and protected by wooden splints, and a crowd behind them watches as the judges rule.

The first heyday of swordplay as exhibition was, of course, the gladiatorial sport of sword fighting in ancient Rome, where many a soldier fenced with a stick whose points were covered by a ball. Militarist Flavius Vegetius Renatus wrote a treatise in which he suggested that good swordsmanship depended on great athleticism, that a great athlete would always shine in any hand-to-hand combat, especially where swords were used, and that the sword was always more effective when used in thrusting rather than cutting motion. Julius Caesar established a gladiatorial school in Campania, and as far as one can tell from images carved on lamps, from toys of the era and from other anthropological remains, gladiators were regarded as rock stars are today, revered, adored and followed with great enthusiasm by throngs of fans. The combat was very real, often deadly, but the goal was always to entertain the spectators with a well-fought bout.

At the "ludi," as the games were called, gladiatorial combatants often fought in pairs, with a referee between them. The rules emanated from the reigning dictator, and the swordsmen were governed by very specific, very strict rules. "Gladiatorem in arena cepere consilium," defined the role of the gladiator; "the gladiator only reveals himself in the arena." In the fight, they would parry and thrust, and the physicians who were appointed to the games specialized in treating wounds caused by sword and trident. Over time, the sword fighting was so popular that it became commonplace among the nobility as well. Swordsmanship was not yet a sport, but combat was "performed" for the entertainment of Coliseum crowds.

After the fall of the Roman Empire – a fall attributed at least in part to the superior swordsmanship of the so-called barbarians – the sword became a part of the romance and the propaganda of war making. Swords became the symbols of their owners' power and majesty, and the medieval knights endowed them with magical, mystical qualities that reflected the attributes to which the knights aspired. The swords often bore names that embodied the hopes and the dreams of the men who carried them.

In the epic poem *Beowulf*, written sometime between the 8th and 11th Century (AD), the warrior Beowulf declares, "With Hrunting I shall gain glory or die." Hrunting is Beowulf's sword, "his best friend, ancient treasure/work of giants' warrior's joy/No lovelier treasure was there known." But here were the seeds of the code of chivalry that carry through to today's fencing: no sword should ever be raised in hatred. A sword was to be used responsibly, and a soldier must fight for honor; a true hero was one who fought only honorably and for the honor of the truth. A true warrior was not a mercenary but rather a champion of a good cause. Because Beowulf allows himself to be angry, because his sword has been tainted by the unsavoriness of Beowulf's friend and rival Unferth, the sword fails, and Beowulf is forced to prove his mettle by fighting with his bare hands.

It became a tradition in epic literature all over the world that swords were named, that they were characters in the heroes' stories. Maybe you have seen the *Lord of the Rings* series in the movies; Frodo has a sword, and the sword's name is Sting. Frodo and Sting follow in the grand manner of all the best medieval and renaissance swordsmen.

In *The Song of Roland*, written sometime between the 12th and 14th C AD, every knight's sword is named, as is every horse; none of the women is named but one. Swords and horses were the extensions of the knights' personae. Charlemagne beheads the Saracen with his sword Joyeuse (Joyous), his nephew Roland carries Durendal (Enduring) into each battle and cuts off the hand of the Saracen general Marsile. Charlemagne and his valiant Joyeuse behead the great Baligant, who must relinquish the sword called Precieuse (Precious). *The Song of Roland* lays the ground work for the Age of Chivalry, of the Knights of the Round Table and the time preceding gun powder when the sword was the ultimate mark of a truly noble knight, a time when the sport of sword play followed the Roman tradition in the arena of public entertainment.

In the Middle Ages, copper and tin were scarce and very expensive, so only the wealthy could afford to carry swords. The sword became the very heart of the code of honor. It represented power that came from within the bearer, the sign of the divine right to call oneself honorable and noble. It was to be drawn only with reason and right, and it was expected to represent intelligence. The cross found on the typical sword of the era had great religious significance; the knight was a holy man, dedicated to God's work.

During this time, new technologies came into being. New weaponry emerged, and while swords primarily remained the possessions of the wealthy, warriors from other classes began to emerge. A long, sharp, narrow-bladed sword was developed for the purpose of reaching into the weak chinks in a knight's armor, and new vocabularies emerged in the military classes.

Among the Scots, a new word entered the vernacular vocabulary. The word "sough" was added to stand for the sound a sword made when it swooshed through the air.

In Great Britain, from the 1100's, through the reign of Henry VIII and his daughter Elizabeth, the art of sword fighting was part of the popular tournaments – called jousts – where knights dueled with one another, often to the death. In France and Italy of the same era, the chaotic and bloody games that dated back to the Latin ludi, were revived, and these evolved into great pageants of armed battles governed by courtesy and the chivalric code. It was still dangerous, and it was still a "game" of death, but protections were being added.

As the tournaments gained popularity, helmets became stronger, and armor became more flexible and had fewer areas of vulnerability. The playing field, the strip of land along which the tournament was held, became a defined space with a regulated size and had a divider built to protect the jousters from falling from their horses.

In Eric et Enide, the first of the five romances that comprise Chretien de Troyes' *Morte d'Arthur*, the author described a bloodless tournament for which knights were trained and which constituted, more than anything else, a convening of the knights of the realm, a brotherhood at arms.

The tournament of the Middle Ages and Renaissance was as popular as hunting and hawking as gentlemen's sports. But the competitions became smaller, more controlled with time. Small teams would practice together and then compete with one another in single and double combats. The strict code of honor grew to include the requirement that each knight raise his visor when meeting one another to reveal their identities, a nicety that carries over in the requirement that every fencer enter the fencing strip with his/her mask tucked under the arm rather than on the face and that each opponent must salute the other before the bout may begin.

Weaponry changed as the games grew in popularity. Preliminary feinting and maneuvering became tactical commonplaces, causing the knights to learn defensive moves that allowed them to evade or duck a blow. The ability to make a quick direction change became a very valuable attribute, and weaponry got lighter and stronger. A fight to the death required that a knight pierce his opponent through a small opening in the armor, so the use of the tip, or point, necessitated that the tip be sharpened. These "games" required great skill and agility, and they are considered the true antecedents of modern fencing.

By the 17th C, armor was discarded, making the swordsmen more vulnerable. But the art of swordplay was increasing in popularity, which necessitated that a tighter code of chivalry was written, and bouts now became popular as "duels of honor" between gentlemen.

As it changed almost every aspect of life, the invention of the printing press in the 15th C spread the art of fencing like a wild fire. Suddenly masters could disseminate ideas more easily and swiftly, and a new era of mastery emerged. A new weapon had been perfected – the rapier was invented, and the first official fencing manual, entitled "I-33" was written by a cloistered monk.

By the middle of the 16th C, the Italians were the acknowledged virtuosi in the art of sword play, and the first language of fencing was Italian. Great schools emerged all over Italy, and manuals appeared on the shelves of noblemen everywhere. Albrecht Dürer – himself the son of a Hungarian goldsmith, by the way – traveled to Italy and made engravings that depicted sword, stave and dagger fights that illustrated a manual translated into German. All over Europe, it was accepted as common knowledge that any gentleman of consequence should know all the turns and terms of swordplay.

A popular book of manners and protocols for gentlemen, by Baldassare Castiglione, characterized the ideal courtier as one who possessed strength, lightness, quickness and the ability to use a sword well. Fencing was no longer simply a martial art desirable for self-defense; it had become an art, desirable for self-identity.

The rapier, which redefined swordplay by being especially well-suited to thrusting, and the choreography described by Italian masters transformed swordplay, and, with the addition of protective buttons on the sword tip, it was now a true sport that was also practiced for self-defense. In Spain, swordplay got very complicated, but the Spaniards developed a rapier that was recognized as the most lethal, most wieldable rapier of all, so that gentlemen all over Europe began carrying Spanish daggers and rapiers.

Henry VIII established the Royal Academy of Fencing to license masters in the "Noble Science of Defense," and it was the only legal school for sword instruction for many years. Swordplay became ubiquitous, bows and arrows were entirely out of fashion, and the English went so far as to create ranks for swordsmen, submitting fencers to various levels of exams to determine their deftness with the weapon. As fencers matriculated from one level to another, they were charged hefty fees and subjected to increasingly rigorous tests. A Master's Prize was established for the highest rank, and competitions were held to determine who was worthy of this prize.

Playing for the prize was a highly physical exhibition, held in the marketplace. All masters competed on a scaffold; there were six weapons, varied over a two-day period, and the display drew a huge crowd. In the plague years, the competitions had to be cancelled, but they recommenced when the threat of plague had passed.

Fencers could now make their living as itinerant performers, similar to jugglers, actors, vagabond musicians.

But fencing was not altogether good for the societies it resided in. As the sport of fencing became ever more popular, and as more and more men (and occasionally women) learned to fence, crime rates increased. There was more street pickpocketing during bouts – thieves capitalized on the distraction provided by the fencing – and even a reprobate would have access to training and could become adroit with a sword. Additionally, many countries still allowed Trials by Combat, and fencers felt that because they were undefeatable they were above the law. They could commit an offense, choose trial by combat and be most likely to beat the opposing swordsman, proving themselves innocent.

Another sword appeared on the scene now, called a sword and buckler. It was heavier than the rapier and considered, therefore, to be more manly. At this point, too, the art of swordplay varied in style. Some fencers preferred the (more Italianate) thrust, emphasizing the sword's point, and others the more (English) defensive use of the edge. The rapier, however, remained popular as a fashion accessory and for its capacity to menace.

Fighting was at times an everyday occurrence. Men skirmished on the streets, in theaters, in the markets. Everyone aspired to swordsmanship, and fencing schools proliferated. Deaths by swordplay rose accordingly. In many European countries, monarchs had to pass laws outlawing public display of swordplay except on the scaffold for exhibition. But they did not prohibit the carrying of swords or attendance at fencing schools, so brawling with swords continued.

In England, for example, it was considered something of a rite of passage in the theater world to kill a man in a duel. Playwright Christopher Marlowe killed a friend in a rapier bout, was arrested and charged with manslaughter, was exonerated and eventually died in a match with another friend. Actor and playwright Ben Jonson was punished for having killed another actor in a duel by having his thumbs branded and his worldly good confiscated. He continued to swordfight and managed to stay just barely clear of the law.

In Germany and France, gangs of sword fighters roamed the streets. In Germany, the moniker "Schwertzucher" was coined and was adopted into English as "Swashbuckler." In Spain and Portugal, youths with swords terrorized their towns and cities. In Italy, the most notorious fencer of all, a Medici family member, introduced the concept of ambush by lying in wait for his prey and attacking from concealment.

Again, now, the art world was involved in the sport of fencing. Benvenuto Cellini, well known goldsmith, sculptor and painter of the 15th C, was admired as much for his swordsmanship as he was for his art. He had a special license to kill with his sword from the Pope, who said that "Men unique in their professions, like Benvenuto, are above the law." Painter Caravaggio, who had no papal protection, killed a man in a swordfight over a tennis match and had to flee Rome but lived and fought on in other Italian cities.

Deadly sword fighting reached its nadir just before the time of William Shakespeare, who, along with Richard Burbage, annexed the Blackfriars School of Fencing to their theater academy. In those days, unruly members of the audience would readily jump onstage to fence along with the actors until an ordinance banned swords in the theater. No one had ever used fencing so well and in so many kinds of plays as did Shakespeare. There are 437 references to swords, five duels. And, of course, in *Hamlet*, the climax of the drama hinges entirely on the outcome of a duel.

But until the 19th C, except on the stage, the duel (from the Latin duello, a combination of the word bellum – war – and duo – 2), a fight between just two swordsmen, was still a deadly business, a fight to the death in most cases. As late as 1884, a duelist was defined as a "professional fighter of duels, an admirer and advocate of the ode duello." But over the second half of the 19th C, the sport of fencing evolved as referees were brought in, rules were enacted that established certain conventions for an artificial, stayed competition, deliberately confined by formal restrictions. But it had taken nearly a thousand years, from the days of King David, of Achilles and Hector, Turnus and Aeneas, for the blood sport to give way to the gentlemanly sport it is today.

In the 1800's, fencing became a very manly sport, called "reconstructed historical fencing. The first modern Olympic Games, in Athens, Greece, had a kind of abbreviated form of fencing, but by 1908, it was a major event at the first London games. Egerton Castle, author of a new fencing manual, was captain of the team, and it was there that this romantic sport – one that simulated the act of armed manslaughter – began to gain popularity on the new world stage.

In France, meanwhile, gentlemen were known to be brash, hot-headed, easily goaded into swordplay. But between the reign of Louis XIII in 1610 and the overthrow of Napoleon in 1815, the violent French nobility had created a gentleman's sport, a kind of marriage between art, science and dance. France was obsessive about swordplay, and during the thirty-five years that Louis XIII reigned, he nurtured the practice rather than outlaw it as he knew he really should. Frenchmen could not get enough of dueling – they fought day and night; they fought anywhere anytime, and it took nearly nothing to set them off. A simple verbal assault could end in bloody mayhem, and it often did. The craze began in Paris but spread quickly to the provinces. Louis XIV attempted to outlaw the duel, but in the 72 years of his reign, the practice became ever more popular. It was in his court that another new weapon – the rapier courte (transition rapier) was introduced.

A new weapon meant the French needed a new kind of fencing school, and Louis XIV provided the coat of arms for the French Academy of Fence. Just as the Académie Française codified the language, literature, math and science of the country, the new French academy established a unique "escrime français," a codifed approach to fencing.

The Fédératon Française d'Escrime defined the way in which the sword should be held, emphasizing a more flexible hold, with thumb and forefinger on either side of the hilt, which allowed a more manageable arm position; movements were more subtle. Five basic steps of drama were integrated into the fence, and French, the language of cooking and gentility, became the language of the fence.

By this time, many conventions of modern cordiality had been adopted from fencing. Today, in western culture, we shake hands to show that we are not reaching for a sword. A Gentleman offers a lady his right arm because he would have carried his sword on his left hip. A man's coat buttons on the right because a duelist would have had to unbutton himself with his left, unarmed, hand.

The sword is heavily endowed with symbolic majesty. It represents justice, power, righteous authority and balance all over the world. In London, the two main parties of the House if Commons are separated by precise lengths of two sword blades, and each Member of Parliament has a locker with a silk loop where he can hang his sword. Kamikaze pilots took swords into their cockpits. Nearly every country's officers carry swords when they are in dress uniform.

Now – A Vigorous but Gentle Game

"A hit. A palpable hit!"

William Shakespeare, **Hamlet**

To this day, fencing is divided into two schools, Italian and French. I began fencing in the Italian style, the style that perfected me was foil fencing, my first weapon. I moved on to the epée and then to the saber, which was the weapon that took me eventually to the Olympics, and then I learned the French style.

When people come to see modern day fencing, they often expect to see something like Clive Owen (in *Elizabeth: The Golden Age*) swinging across a ship's masts, carrying his sword and thrusting every enemy he encounters. But the reality is that while fencing is fast and athletic, it is done on a piste, which is a very contained area, a six-foot-by-forty-foot strip (the area is actually defined metrically as being 1.5-2 meters wide and 14 meters long), made from one of four basic materials: metallic, rubber, aluminum, and fiberglass. The fencing moves so quickly that scoring must be done electronically, by sensors attached that announce the hit by making an audible sound and/or by flashing lights.

I was unusual in the sport of fencing in that in the year preceding the Olympics, when I had been the Israeli Fencing Champion for three consecutive years, I set a record that might never be broken by winning the national championship in all three weapons; most fencers specialize in one from the beginning. The three weapons are the Epee, the Foil and the Saber. Each has its own origins, its own traditions and its own scoring rules.

Épée

The Epée is the result of years of refinement to the Renaissance rapier, the dueling weapon. It is, like the foil, a thrusting sword, a thick blade with a triangle cross section and a groove in the center as well as a large, bell-shaped guard to protect the hand and forearm. Points can be scored by the first hit on any part of the body whatsoever, but only the first hit counts.

Épée

Foil

The Foil is a more complicated weapon. It is light and flexible, and it originated in France as a lighter, thinner departure from the rapier, then called the fleuret. The sword itself is divided into multiple parts, each having a name and a purpose; the Forte and the Foible comprise the blade, which has a button at the very tip. A pad protects the hand and forearm behind the guard, and a wrist strap, known as the Martingale, keeps the long handle from having too wide a latitude. The only valid hit is made when the point of the weapon hits the opponent's body trunk; hits to the abdomen, chest and back will score, but those to the arms, legs and head will not. The fencer must hit the target area and have the right to attack.

Foil

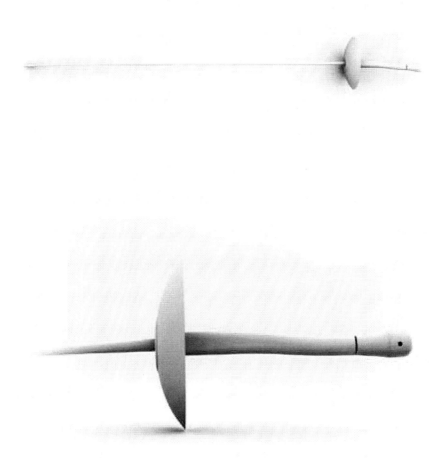

Saber

The saber evolved from the military sword, which was probably brought to Europe by the Turks; and, because it was the sword brought to Hungary in the 19th C by way of the Austrian army, it has always been favored by Hungarian fencers, which is why it was my father's weapon and why I was expected to master the saber as well. It, too, is light and flexible and can both thrust and cut in order to make its hits. With the saber, a fencer hits with edge cuts or point thrusts and hits are only scored above the opponent's waist. Any hit above the waist – including hits to arms and head – counts as a scorable hit. The fencer who hits the target and has the "right to attack" is the one who scores.

Saber

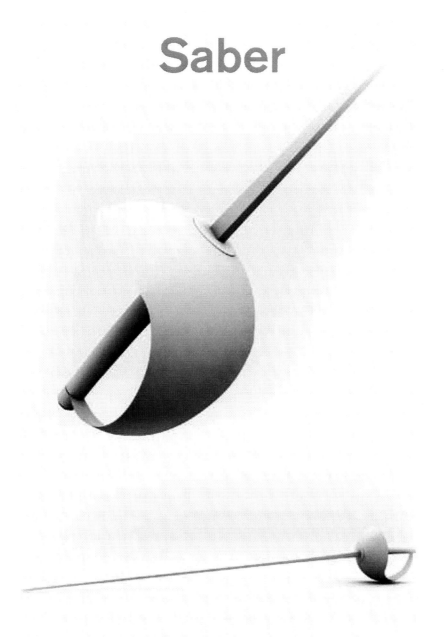

Uniform

Modern fencing is a true meshing of art and science, and nowhere is that more apparent than in the uniform worn by every competitive fencer. Fencing jackets, breeches, and underarm protectors were traditionally made of cotton or nylon, but following the so-called Smirnov incident – a freak accident, where fencer Vladimir Smirnov was killed at the 1982 World Championships, when his opponent's blade penetrated the mesh of his mask and pierced his brain – Kevlar and then a newer and stronger synthetic called Dyneema were incorporated.

The full outfit, designed entirely for protection, can vary, depending on the weapon the fencer uses. The epee and foil costume includes of the form-fitting jacket that also covers the groin are with a strap (un croissard) that fits between the legs; the saber fencer's jacket has no strap, and the jacket ends at the fencer's waist.

Around the collar of every fencer's jacket, a gorget, a small folded piece of fabric, is sewn to protect the wearer from having his opponent's point piercing his neck. A plastron, or underarm protector is worn under the jacket for extra protection on the sword arm side and upper arm; the jacket may have no armpit seam, as a seam would be a weakness where a blade might find a way into the fencer's body.

The weapon arm is gloved, and a thick gauntlet prevents the blade from going up the sleeve to cause injury. Breeches or knickers, held in place by suspenders, knee-length or thigh high socks, flat-soled shoes and a mask with a bib round out the uniform of the fencer.

The shoes are reinforced along the inside of the back of the foot and along the heel to prevent erosion from lunging, and most modern masks have see-through visors.

In fencing, it is absolutely true that clothes make the man – or the woman – and they keep fencing from being, as it began, a blood sport.

Mask

Fencing is definitely a sport that has its own language as well as its traditions. Each individual game is called a bout. The object of a bout is to score a specific number of points on an opponent before s/he can score them first. Each touch, within the definition of where and when a touch is legal, is a point. A match consists of three three-minute intervals.

When a fencer has the right to hit, s/he has the right of way. This is perhaps the most difficult concept in fencing and was originated to prevent simultaneous attacks by two fencers. The rule of right of way establishes which fencer is offensive and which defensive, and the call is made by the referee; epée fencers do not use the right of way, as they are bound by the "first hit" rule, which only scores the very first hit in each attack.

For the untrained eye, following fencing is dizzying, and understanding a few of the words/concepts helps to make some sense. The attacker thrusts. The fencer being attacked uses a parry , a defensive motion to deflect the opponent's blade, after which the attacker may make a riposte, a return attack. The adversaries alternate as offensive or defensive fighters, and the referee stops the bout whenever a hit is made. Without electronic scoring devices, the judgment of a score is entirely up to the referee, who describes the hit and determines whether it is to be awarded the touch. During the bout, fencers will seek distance for defense but will seek to close the distance for attack; often an attack will be faked in order that the fencer may judge his/her opponent's reaction. Both distance and elimination of distance are affected through footwork, which is dancelike it its swift litheness.

More than most athletes, fencers rely on psychological strength for success. They fight with a constant awareness of the "tactical wheel" (also called a "tactical tree"), a theory that every tactic will defeat the one before as it will be defeated by the one that comes thereafter if done right. The fencer must assume an opponent's move while simultaneously planning his/her own, choosing what moves to make as one goes along. That's a lot of thinking while wielding a sword, dancing defensively and aggressively and trying not to be hit. Like a very skillful chess player, I had to constantly know – or intuit – what my opponent would do next so that I could deliberately set up m maneuver so that I could bait and trap and defeat my opponent. I had to know where his weakest and strongest points were, and I had to make an accurate assessment. This is why having a practice partner like Yoram is so important. The perfect partner should approximate the competition and be someone the fencer can get to know well, someone the fencer can size up astutely.

It was always my goal to make my opponent do what I wanted him to do so that I could position him to lose the bout. Of course, his intention was exactly the same as mine. The fencer who was best able to psych out an opponent would always be the fencer who won the fight.

A common error young fencers make is watching their opponent's body. A good fencer watches his/her opponents' eyes. In the eyes, I can see every movement before it is made. The eyes give automatic orders to the brain what to do. Work smarter, move the feet better, appel faster. Eyes are the human camera and transmit an automatic message.

When I arrived in Munich for the Olympics, I was among an elite sampling of athletes chosen by the resident physicians to do a study of the overall health, strength, speed and agility of the athletes. After being poked and prodded and given every kind of test imaginable, I was singled out as one of the strongest, fastest, most agile athletes among the delegations. That didn't surprise me, as I had had to train by running and dancing and working out in a number of ways and developing my reflexes, and as proud as I was to be recognized as such, I knew that being the strongest, fastest, most agile athlete would not win me a medal. I had to be mentally stronger by far than my opponents, and in a world arena where so much distraction lurked around every corner, that was the tallest order of all.

CHAPTER 10

The Swordsman in Me

"Surfers believe that somewhere out there rolls that perfect wave; Reichean sexologists seek the prefect orgasm; physicists long for everything to be reducible to one equation; executioners spoke of the perfect beheading. Any skillful activity invites the notion of its distillation into an absolute ideal. For swordsmen, this has manifested itself in the quest for the perfect thrust."

Richard Cohen, **By the Sword**

The first round of fencing matches at Munich

Dan on his balcony in Connollystrasse overlooking Olympic village

I think I have always known there is no such thing as that absolute ideal, a perfection that can leave a man breathless and then hopeless because he could never hope to achieve it again. How could the perfect thrust be possible, when every move, every breath on the piste depends on so many variables, most of them out of my own control. I can put myself into another man's thinking and attempt to psyche him out, but I can never KNOW what is in his head. I can plan my movements down to the minutest detail, but I cannot foresee with absolute certainty where I will have to be or how I will have to move in order to protect myself from his choices. So, in many ways, the sword has made me a realist. I know what is; I change what I can and accept what I can't, and I am pretty good at knowing which is which. Much of that has come from this sport I have been engaged in my whole life. And from the example my father set.

No matter what adversity my father had to face, he simply took it in his stride and did his best to remedy what he could. He was a great athlete and a champion fencer. There's a special corner in my home for all his medals – even those he won in gymnastics before his knees began to give him trouble, giving him the incentive to try fencing.

It was at a European competition in Yugoslavia in 1938, that my father received a telegram from a friend warning him to stay in Yugoslavia, that it was unsafe to return to Hungary. He never did return to Hungary, but he went instead to Palestine where he pioneered the new country of Israel. Except for his parents and his older sister, who came to join us in Israel in 1950, his family was erased; there was nothing left for him in Europe. He found himself a fencing group and worked his way back up to championship status, and he never complained that he had lost his chance to compete in an Olympic Games.

Fencing makes one strong in so many ways.

From the time I was very young, I worked on all the many skills I needed to become a world-class fencer. I ran every day on the beach, along the sand dunes, up hills, through fields. I thought of myself as a gladiator, but a gladiator who needed to make his legs absolutely elastic. I found a universal gym and trained myself to use each of the stations, exercising every muscle, doing the whole circuit many times. I did push-ups and crunches, developed my speed and reflexes, trained my eyes to be fast, and worked on making my hands and legs very quick. I played a lot of ping-pong, which is good for perfecting reaction time and for building speed. I also played silly kids' games that I knew would make me fast – I chased cats and improvised in every way possible I could think of to make me faster.

As a teenager, I was up at 6 every day and didn't sleep again till 1AM. I enjoyed my life, and I didn't need to sleep. My best friend used to chide me, "Oh, Dani, keep on doing that, and you'll have a heart attack before you are 40." Ironic really. He never worked out and got plenty of rest, and he was dead of a coronary before he turned 39.

I never ate a lot, but I ate well. I still eat everything! As a fencer, I had to be a bit careful because I do love food – especially things like ice cream and rich desserts – and had a tendency to get a bit pudgy. But it was all part of my extraordinary love for living. Everything about life engaged me, especially things like food that feel so good. Whenever we would travel to competitions in Europe, we would go out to eat, and if there were ten of us ordering t-bone steaks, I would suck the marrow out of everyone else's bones. I was like that about everything, including my training.

I was talented, ambitious, and I liked to fence all the best fencers in all three weapons. It was fun for me to compete, no matter which weapon, and I could fence against anyone. I never limited myself so I was quite self-satisfied, fencing all the time with anybody who would fence. The only competitors I did not face were women, but sometimes in practice, I would fence with the women foil fencers. Today women use all three weapons, but until thirty or forty years ago, they only fenced with foils, and they were good.

Even as a child, I was no stranger to tragedy. I mourned with my father for his many losses, which affected me deeply, and I, too, lost very close friends at very critical junctures in my life. I believe that sustaining those pains certainly helped to strengthen me, but I owe my true inner stamina to fencing.

I am not sure had I been trained in any other discipline I would have been able to recover from the terror of Munich. All the years of learning to think for others, to take myself out of my own body in order to anticipate an opponent's moves, all the ways in which I had to build mental callouses got me through the worst. My family, my friends, my deep spirituality were all fundamentally crucial to my recovery, but my greatest font of survivability comes from my sport.

I honestly believe that it is because of the grounding I had in fencing that I am able to be happy once again. I no longer fence, but I had the physical, emotional and intellectual fortitude to turn my attention to an equally fascinating sport and to apply myself in that area. Today I am a golfer, and I am a pretty good one at that. It is a relaxing sport, a real release for me, and I credit fencing with preparing me to excel as a golfer.

Six years ago, my wife's cousin Neville, visiting from South Africa, invited me to play a round of golf with him. I was at first completely underwhelmed; it never occurred to me that I might take an interest in golf. But Neville goaded, coaxed, prodded until out of desperation to get him off my back, I took a one-hour lesson. I could not get over how much I loved it. It suited me perfectly and seemed in many ways to be close to fencing.

Golf, too, requires complete coordination in all parts of the body – legs, hips, hands being able to move in sync with one another. The momentum is in the timing; when to hit the ball and how to hit the ball depend entirely on one another. I fell in love with golf, and, after Neville returned to his home country, I continued to pursue it on my own. I played every day, and, at 57, becoming a master of a new endeavor was not easy, but I persevered. I joined a club, and I went every evening after work. In all kinds of weather, I spent at least two hours on the driving range or at the links. Results came very quickly. I was soon one of the few people in my club with a handicap of 10 or less. No one who knows about me and fencing is surprised, but I still marvel at my great good fortune in finding the sport, which has also given me a new team.

Every Saturday morning seven other men and I, who call ourselves the Footwedge Warriors, go out to the links to play at the Gaash Golf Club, outside of Tel Aviv. We have become good friends, and we socialize together with our families. We even had t-shirts made with our logo on them. I am delighted, and it all keeps me young. My own partner, my attorney Jonathan, could be my son but treats me as an equal. It's a great joy to be part of this, and I owe it in large measure to my fencing.

CHAPTER 11

Peace in Our Time – Life Goes On

I know of course; it's simply luck
That I've survived so many friends.

> *Bertolt Brecht*

Top My children Pazit, Arik, Meir
Middle Yoram *(center)* and his daughters Roni *(left)* and Libi *(right)*
Bottom Pazit, Arik, Arik's wife Dafi, Meir

After the shock, the horror, the disappointment and the betrayals of Munich and its aftermath, I realized something terribly important. I am still the same person who went to Munich, though I have grown immeasurably. I am still the man who loves music and art, who revels in food and dance, who adores his family and is passionate about his country. I have learned things I may not have wanted to know, and I have had to reach inside myself for resources I thought I had lost, but I'm still here, and I'm still in love with living.

I remember an incident that happened many years ago, something I had forgotten until I began to speak about Munich, and I think I remembered it then because it had special meaning to me in the wake of the tragedy.

I spoke German before I spoke Hebrew. My parents worked, and my mother's parents, survivors from Vienna, Austria, lived with us and watched over me during the day. They spoke only German, so at home we all spoke German, and I didn't learn Hebrew really till I went to school. As a young man, I studied and lived in Germany a few times, and my German is good enough for any German.

During one of my many visits to Germany, I was on the train, and the conductor came and said I had the wrong ticket, that I was cheating. The ticket was for a visitor, and I was, as far as he could tell, clearly a native. I said that wasn't true, that I was a tourist, and he laughed at me. It was a great compliment, of course, but I had to prove to him that I was telling the truth. I showed him my Israeli passport, and he reacted immediately, was terribly embarrassed. I guessed that he was about the right age to have been around during the Third Reich, and I could see that he went to pieces over the revelation that not only was I a foreigner, but I was a Jew. For the rest of the trip, he bent over backward to please me, soliciting me for requests, begging me to allow him to do something for me. I, of course, became just as embarrassed, and the trip was excruciatingly uncomfortable.

People who meet those of us who have survived unscathed have no idea what to say, how to treat us. We don't fit their bill to be considered survivors, really; we have no visible scars, no harrowing tales of being held at gunpoint before bolting through a dark, concrete forest. Their discomfort makes them almost resent us, as they don't know what we might want from them, don't know what we might expect. We either become the object of their derision or the target of their abject pity.

I didn't do anything wrong by running away from Apartment 2 that terrible day in September. I did not betray my friends, and not a single one of them died in my place. It was not my time, not my karma to suffer and die with them. It's as simple as that.

But that is not a simple conclusion to arrive at. It takes time and work and a lot of love. I was fortunate. I had all three.

My family was no stranger to adversity; we were and are all survivors. My grandparents survived WWII and the relocation process, and my parents managed to feed us and sustain us despite the terrible shortages of the 40's and 50's and the Arab attacks immediately following the partition. My maternal grandfather's most cherished dream was to pray at the Kotel, the Western Wall on the Temple Mount, in the Old City of Jerusalem. His dream was never realized because he died just before the Six-Day War, but at least my parents saw Israel reunited with Jerusalem.

With my brother Yoram and my father, I built a very successful print business out of the one my father originated before Independence, near Jaffa, in the days when doing business in the "Arab section," at the street that divided Jaffa from Tel Aviv, was very dangerous. My father was ambitious and devoted himself to making the business work there, despite the risk to his life.

I always felt honored that I got my father's hands and that I, too, am able to use them creatively, which was as much an asset in the printing and graphics business as it was in fencing. When I came of age, I gave as much of myself to learning the trade, being a craftsman, as I ever did to fencing. Yoram, who is a far better salesman than I, put himself whole-heartedly into creating a network, of making our business desirable to other businesses, and together we prospered for thirty-six years.

Yoram never complained that he didn't get his chance at the Olympics. When I left fencing, he left with me, and he never looked back, never questioned the decision to do so. He, too, had inherited great strength from our parents. For years, my mother was crazy with worry that he didn't marry, but he always did things at his own pace, and at 43, he did marry -- a New Yorker named Karmit. My mother died before the wedding, but by then she knew he was happy. Today he and his teen-age daughters Libi, who is in the military, and Roni, who is still in school live near by so we are able to see one another often.

My father was not with me for long after Munich, but he helped me through a lot before he died in 1977 at the very young age of 60; I had my mother till 1989. Together they helped to focus me on what was important: my family, my personal life and pursuits. And now, as I see the fruits of my labors, I am very proud.

My oldest son Meir, my father's namesake, is an electronics engineer who has recently become a high school teacher. My second son Arik is in school, studying drama and film; he hopes to be a screenwriter, to make movies and exercise his enormous creativity. Arik's wife Dafi works in television, and she has brought me great joy. Of course, the light of my life is still my daughter Pazit, who specializes in insurance law and plans very soon to complete her master's degree.

Adele, the indomitable woman to whom I am married, is still nursing, and she, too, could write a book. For years, she worked in the emergency room of Ichilov Hospital, Tel Aviv's main hospital, which serves the entire metropolitan area, and she had some harrowing experiences. She was on duty when Former Prime Minister Yitzhak Rabin was assassinated in 1995. No one realized who he was when they brought him in; it was only after Adele and her colleagues had taken him into the trauma unit that his identity was discovered. When he died, everyone was shocked. The experience was shattering to the staff, and Adele was deeply affected.

The emergency room at Ichilov was like a microcosm of all the troubles in Israel, and catastrophes daily found their way to Adele's care. Suicide bombers, big bus bombing victims, accident victims – all the broken people of our nation – needed her care. She worked long hours on her feet, exerting herself physically and emotionally, with little rest; even when she was off-duty, she was on call, and she never escaped.

Today, Adele has discovered a whole new professional perspective. She re-trained as an In vitro fertilization (IVF) nurse and has found once again the omnipresent smile that made me fall in love with her. In her IVF clinic, she is surrounded by hope and promise; miracles happen often there. That has given her a whole new sense of her own worth, and I am very proud of her and relieved to see the joy return to her heart. She doesn't share my love of golf, but she has found her own sport: Bridge, which she plays often and plays well. She does like to travel with me, however, and we take our vacations with my golf partner Jonathan and his wife. We have a splendid life together.

CHAPTER 12

Finding My Voice

Now we have found our homes again,

Our bellies are full,

We're through telling the story.

It's time.

       Primo Levi, **Reveille**

Meir and Dan at the Olympic Village in 2011

Adele and Dan Alon

For thirty-four years I was silent about the 1972 massacre at the Munich Olympics. I was struck dumb by the experience, shattered in ways I could not understand, and I had no capacity to tell the story. I was stunned into silence, unable to speak of the events I witnessed.

People have said to me that I must have felt guilty, and perhaps that was why I could not speak. That's not really it. I mean, no sane person walks away from a disaster thinking, "I wish I had been the one who died." It is human nature, rather, to gasp with relief, to sigh with gratitude that life will go on. Instinct impels the survivor to glory in the moment of great good fortune. But then, in the ensuing weeks, the shock, terror and rejoicing give way to pain as the survivor encounters some of the gruesome truths that had been obscured by the relief. And then it takes a very long time to sort through all of it and come back with some sense of what it all might mean, or at least with a knowledge that what I have to say about it matters.

I got little recognition for where I had been in the aftermath of Munich, and when people did talk to me about it, they talked to me like I did something heroic. But that made me feel even more inadequate. I was bewildered by some overwhelming questions like, "Why didn't I fight back?" "Why me and not them?" Recovering from the ordeal, leaving the less fortunate in untimely graves, I found myself buried in stultifying grief and self-doubt. "I am such a coward," I would tell myself. "I could have done something, but instead I just ran. Why do I deserve to live?"

My turmoil put me in a state of lonely silence, silence that insulated me from my nagging sense of failure, especially after I allowed my distrust and anxiety to coerce me out of fencing. Eventually, however, I came to realize that I could never recover unless I could find the words to share, the strength to speak up, to tell the story so that others would know what happened and understand the pain, so that somewhere sometime a similar event might be averted.

I didn't have that revelation on my own. I didn't find the motivation to articulate the notion to myself until I was wrenched from my reticence by others far wiser than I.

It began when my son Arik was in England. He went to a screening of Steven Spielberg's *Munich* at a Chabad center there, and afterward, in the course of the discussion led by Rabbi Eli Brackman, Arik shared what he knew about my experiences at Munich, which, honestly was very little; I had never really told my children what I saw or did, and Arik only knew what he had learned from the media and that I was somehow involved.

The rabbi was flabbergasted. Rarely does anyone come forward who was in Munich, and most people don't even realize that there were athletes were in the house who survived without ever being taken hostage. The rabbi begged Arik to call me, which he did, and right then and there I got my first invitation to share my story. "Come to London, Dan," suggested the good rabbi. "Your expenses will be paid, and you'll have a place to stay. Please come."

My initial reaction was to retreat. I could not imagine that anyone would care at all to hear my story. But the rabbi insisted. He said that like any survivor's tale, mine could be instructive. "You will be a shaliach, Dani," proclaimed the rabbi. "A messenger. Through you others will know what it means to survive. Through you others will know how to find the bravery within to face the dangers of our modern world."

His argument was compelling, so I packed a bag, and that very week I spoke at Cambridge and at Oxford for the Chabad communities there. At that very first speaking engagement, I was approached by a member of the audience, a psychiatrist, who told me I should be telling my story as often as possible. "This is a good thing you are doing, Dani," the doctor said. "Not just for the listeners but for you as well. You are haunted by the ghosts of your experience, and speaking far and wide will help you exorcise your dybbuks."

I could see that what he said had merit. I already was beginning to feel somewhat better about it all just from the reception I got there. The students and the others were very moved by my story, and they wrote about me in their newspapers, in their online publications, in their emails, etc. Pretty soon, I had my own presence on the web, and Rabbi Shua Rosenstein, the visionary Chabad rabbi at Yale University in New Haven, read about me and invited me to the United States.

I spoke at Yale, and afterward, Rabbi Rosenstein and his wife Sara invited me to join him and his students at Shabbat dinner. It was a very moving evening; I felt as though I were with family, and I have come to regard the rabbi, his wife and his children as just that, family.

Rabbi Rosenstein became like my advocate, almost like my agent, and as a result, I have been welcomed in places I would never have expected to find such eager listeners.

Thanks to the wise and entrepreneurial rabbi, I have taken my story all over the world – to the UK, Taiwan, India, Continental Europe, the US and elsewhere – and everywhere I go, I am honored by the respect and sympathy extended to me, and I begin to feel the demons leave me. In Phoenix, in 2007, I was the keynote speaker at their Maccabiah games, and I addressed a crowd of thousands of athletes and their parents in the Phoenix Coliseum; afterwards, the youngsters came to me for autographs as though I were a rock star.

I still battle beasts within. They come at me when I least expect them. Once, fifteen years ago, I went to Munich with my brother Yoram, and we stayed in a small hotel in Germany I had stayed in many times and whose proprietor I knew. The hotel was for businesspeople only, and it was normally closed on the weekend. In order to accommodate us, the landlady, who lived in a flat on the first floor, gave us a key to the hotel and reminded us that we would be the only people in the place after Friday morning. That Friday night, Yoram and I went out with some German friends, and when we came back from our evening of drinking and dancing, we saw, lurking by the entrance, two men speaking Arabic. They opened the door with a key and went to the second floor, which I thought was terribly suspicious, as Yoram and I thought we had the only key. I went to the landlady and woke her, telling her what I had seen. "Oh," she said. "They're just businessmen from Morocco, and I let them stay here tonight." I reminded her that I was a survivor of the Munich Massacre, and she said, "Oh, that's right. I agree that perhaps we should call the police," and she did.

Within five minutes, the place was swarming with police. The whole village was awake, and there were armed cops everywhere, with sirens and blaring and rifles cocked and ready for action. One thing about the German police, they learn from the past! The two men were taken into custody for interrogation, and we waited at the hotel for word from the police. Toward morning, they came and told us that the men were harmless businessmen, and I was terribly sorry, but I still wasn't confident enough to go back inside my room to sleep; I went to my friend's house to sleep instead. I was embarrassed to know that my paranoia had caused such an uproar, and I apologized profusely. Everyone understood and was very kind, but I would have been mortified except that I remembered how not speaking up at Munich had helped to cause a far worse scenario.

Another time, in another German city, the rabbi put me in a small hotel near to the Chabad Center. He thought I would prefer the ease of being close to where I was to speak and where I would find my community. But as happened before in other German hotels, everyone in that hotel looked like Arabs; the receptionist, the bellboy, the management all spoke Arabic. I froze when I entered, then turned around, without putting my suitcases down, and walked to the rabbi's office where I asked that I immediately be moved me to a larger hotel downtown, a hotel run by Israelis, where I found myself in the company of many Israelis and Jews from around the world. I felt much better there.

With each passing year, things get a little better. I am calmer, I don't hear gunfire every time a car backfires, and I don't see Arabs lurking in every shadow. But it's still hard.

Last summer, I returned to Munich on a business trip, and, since my elder son Meir was with me, I suggested we travel to the Olympic Village so he could see first hand what it looked like. Just as I had in 2004, I found a taxi driver to take us there, but this time I had him leave us so we could walk around freely.

The village is bustling with activity; there is no real evidence of the terrible thing that happened there. We walked around and made our way to 31 Connolly Street, where we found the plaque placed in front of our quarters. The plaque is written in German and in Hebrew, a matter-of-fact reminder of how painfully simply death and destruction were able to overtake us. I broke down and cried like a baby; my son had to call Adele for help. I was so distraught, I could not move, could not see, could hardly breathe.

Thank goodness for Adele. She talked me back to life. She reminded me how fortunate I am, how deeply rooted I am in this beautiful life we have made together, and she begged me to forgive myself and let the pain, the anger, the torture go. I stayed on the phone with her for what felt like a very long time, and when I hung up, I felt like a burden had been lifted from me, as though I were somehow reborn. I can't articulate exactly what the feeling was, but I knew for the first time in nearly forty years that I would be okay, that we would be okay. I truly am...free at last.

****

Still, when I close my eyes, I see that plaque on the apartment building, and I still feel the sting of the tremendous loss we suffered that awful day.

The team of the State of Israel stayed in this building during the 20th Olympic Summer Games from 21 August till 5 September,1972. On 5 September, Moshe Weinberg, Yossef Romano, Ze'ev Friedman, David Berger, Yakov Springer, Eliezer Halfin, Yossef Gutfreund, Kehat Shorr, Mark Slavin, Andre Spitzer, and Amitzur Shapira died a violent death. Honor to their memory.

CHAPTER 13

Relearning to Breathe

After the end of the world

After death

I found myself in the midst of life

Creating myself

Building life

      Tadeuz Rozewicz, **After the End of the World**

Meir, Arik, and Adele

Endre Kabos, Hungary's most celebrated fencer, who won championships at the Los Angeles and Berlin Olympics, was presented, in 1936, with a very special recognition trophy by the Jewish community of Budapest, and after the war, in an effort to finance their immigration to the United States, the Kabos family survivors sold all the fencer's medals and trophies. They did manage to get to the US, and I would very much like to know where they are today because, through that special trophy, I am linked to them.

After the 1967 6-Day War in Israel, there were many difficulties between Israel and Eastern Europe. Much of Eastern Europe, including Hungary, was aligned with Syria and others and broke off relations with Israel. The Israeli ambassador, completing a bid for reconciliation and about to leave Hungary, was browsing in a flea market one afternoon and found the trophy that had been forged for Kabos by the Jewish community. He brought it back to Israel, where he presented it to the Hungarian émigré community. Sometime later, the community leadership hosted a fencing competition in Kabos' honor, and they offered that special trophy as the prize to the first place winner, and I was he.

I still own that trophy, which is very dear to me. But I would love to get it back to the Kabos family someday. I hope perhaps they will read this book and contact me so I can send it to them. This becomes more compelling a desire to me as I get further and further from the Munich experience and as time and forgiveness help to heal my soul.

I have come to realize how important it is to look the past squarely in the eye and make peace with it. Now that I've had some time to come out of my self-torture, I know that everything I have said, everything I have written about that day in Munich will be important to my descendants and even to my countrymen. I hope some day that my grandchildren will have my trophies, my book, my swords, and I hope they will be able to appreciate how much of me is in each of them.

*****

A few years ago, when I had begun to make the rounds speaking across the US about Munich, my wife's cousin Lynda, Neville's sister, came to meet us at the airport when Adele and I flew to Los Angeles for a speaking engagement there. After I spoke, Lynda asked the facilitators of the program to arrange for me to attend a special event, a reunion of Auschwitz survivors at the Beverly Hills Hotel. We went immediately to that party, where we found a few hundred people, the old survivors, their children and grandchildren and friends.

There was an orchestra there, and we danced and laughed and had a wonderful time talking to some of the people, just mingling. After dinner, the President of the club, the event organizer, stood up and told the crowd he had a big surprise for them, and he introduced me. They cheered wildly as I walked up to the podium and told them I was happy to be there, to share the solidarity of survivorship with them. Just then the orchestra began to play Israeli music, and the survivors lifted me up like a bridegroom onto a chair, which they carried about the room, dancing with me, cheering for me.

After, when I told them tearfully how grateful I was, they wept, and then one by one they told me how happy they were to have me there, so grateful that I had come to share the afternoon with them.

That night I felt cleansed. I felt whole for the first time since the massacre. I knew that I was, like them, a survivor, and I was no longer afraid to be grateful. Finding my voice freed my soul.

CHAPTER 14
Epilogue: Reunion

Dan interviewed for 2012 Munich reunion documentary

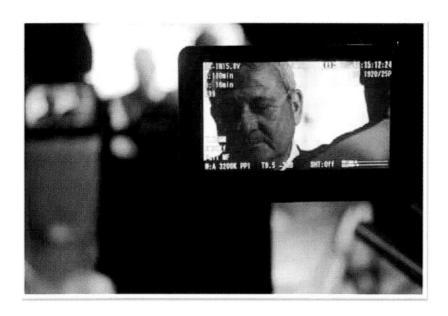

In February, 2012, all of us survivors -- and just we alone -- returned to Munich together to participate in a documentary that was co-produced by the Israeli History Channel and the German Biography Channel. There, with my fellow athletes, I finally achieved the peace I have been seeking all these years.

Like me, the others have been fairly silent about what happened to us. Finding the right words, placing the exact emotions are hard enough, but we all shared the sense that no one really wanted to hear what we had to say. World sympathy was directed to the families of the slain and rightly so; no one ever asked any of us, "What was it like?" or "What did you feel when you walked away?" or "How are you holding up with the stress of the horror you lived through still in your stomach?"

All of a sudden, in Munich last February, those of us who had been in the shadows all these years became the subject of great concern, great interest. The producers flew us with our spouses to Munich and put us up in a fine hotel. Together we visited the stadium and the apartment at Connolly Street, and we went to the Jewish community and had dinner with them. All the while, cameras were rolling, and reporters were recording what we were saying, how we were reacting; they asked us for our opinions, our hopes, our disappointments, our dreams. We were recognized as survivors at last.

The production staff set up a soundproof television studio inside the Olympic stadium, and each of us was taken into the room for a private session with the reporters. We were given time and encouragement to tell everything we could remember about that terrible day, about the aftermath, about the overall experience, and it felt so validating that we all walked away feeling renewed.

Together we were able to face the past and resolve to heal the future. We discussed with one another what we had thought were private memories -- so many things I had feared had happened only in my own tortured mind -- and were comforted to know that these were actually memories we shared with one another.

Even if a few of the details did not match (I learned, for example, that a memory I had of climbing over a fence to get out of my apartment had not happened), it was okay. We were able to justify for one another that it all really happened, that we had all lived through this horror, but that none of us had anything to be ashamed of for having survived.

And best of all, we were able to talk about the men who were murdered, men who were our friends and colleagues, about whom we have had very little opportunity to speak so openly since they were taken from us. I found I had a lot to say about Andrei Spitzer, whom I loved like a brother, and looking into the camera and remembering aloud was empowering. When I talked with others, especially to Yehuda, who was our third musketeer, I found myself laughing as I remembered, in a way laughing with Andrei for the first time in nearly forty years.

Each of us has a singular regret, a moment that makes us cringe with fear, shrivel with remorse, and we were able to share those with one another. Mine was always a nagging voice that said I should not have run away that morning, that I should have gone in to do battle with the terrorists. I know now, better than ever, how futile, how useless that would have been, and I no longer question that what I did was what I should have done. It feels good to know, in the end, I am here because I am meant to be here, and it is simply God's will.

Perhaps not all our moments of regret are erased. Some of them will continue to nag at us all our lives, I suppose. Zelig Struch, my marksman roommate, has often told me that he, just like Henry Hershkowitz, wishes we had listened to him and taken his rifle to go after the gunmen. He said it again at the reunion, and I believe he will say it whenever we meet. "Until today, I wonder whether I did the right thing when I didn't shoot the terrorists' leader, who was only a few meters away from me," he says.

I am sure he knows it wouldn't have helped, but he will always second-guess himself nonetheless.

****

Twenty years ago, I was in Vienna, and when it came time to fly back, I queued up, along with my fellow El Al travelers, in a line to await a security check. The probing, poking, prodding by the guards were exhaustive -- there were many Austrian airport guards as well as El Al personnel there to go through our bags, to pat us down individually, to ask us questions, to thoroughly check us out.

I looked across the way, just a few meters from where we were undergoing the humiliation of the search, and there I saw another queue, this one of passengers preparing to board a Saudi airplane bound for Damascus. There was no security there, and no one was poked or prodded or searched; they simply showed their passports and entered their aircraft. The travelers watched us undergo our ordeal, and they laughed at us. They pointed and made jokes, loudly deriding us for having to suffer the indignity of the security check.

Since then I have traveled extensively all over the world, and as the anti-terror operation intensifies with every trip I make, the business of it takes ever more time. There have been several instances where I nearly missed a flight because I was trying to get through security. Yet it is still true that if you fly in and out of Arab countries, the security is lax, and travelers go freely from city to city and country to country without the degradation of security checks.

The very countries that support terrorism, who fund it and who harbor its perpetrators are not taking precautions to protect their citizens. Why? Because their citizens have nothing to fear. Public opinion is neutral; the people can afford to be complacent. No one threatens to blow up an Emirates aircraft or a Syrian airport. There is no need to check for explosives, for knives concealed in shoes, for liquids designed to crash a plane, and commuters simply fly unperturbed. Legislators have no need to make laws requiring search and seizure on planes because the people there don't demand it.

So I wonder. Perhaps we are going about this all wrong. Perhaps by defending ourselves against terrorism, we are perpetuating it. So long as we are prepared for it, it will always be there.

It occurs to me that when we bomb Gaza, we have no real hope that we will gain anything. We don't really seek to harm or kill or make any headway. We do it because we want people to feel insecure, to put pressure on their government to force changes in policy that will benefit us. We understand that the only way to affect change is to instill fear in the people's hearts so that they will pressure their government to do what is needed to protect them.

What if groups from our side of the fence were to levy threats on our enemy's modes of travel? What if there were an organization of Americans akin to the PLO who would place cells in strategic Arabic areas about the world and threaten their safety by smuggling bombs into the buildings they frequent? What if we were to send messages that made them go into red alert and put them at risk? In other words, what if we were to put THEM in harm's way along with us?

I know it's not a very gentle notion, and I am sure most people would think me a bit nuts to suggest it. It seems to me that by being defensive, we encourage terrorism; perhaps it requires some offensive measures to eradicate it. At least by launching an offensive, we would show them that they are vulnerable, and they will begin to pressure their governments to stop the terror and drive terror from their own lives.

In the final analysis, I would love to believe that I might have a grandchild who will go to the Olympics some day. And I would love to believe that he or she will be free from the possibility of such a menace. I dream of a world without violence, and I believe the world should take whatever measures possible to build a world without dread.

Afterword

In May, 2007, after completing a speaking engagement in Berlin, a Mitzvah Van* from the local Chabad organization came early in the morning to take me to the airport. In the van, my driver was playing a CD by Rabbi Shlomo Carlebach, the singing rabbi, and just as we got to the Brandenburg Gate, my favorite song began. "Am Israel Chai!" (Israel lives!), sang the Rebbe. I asked the driver to turn on the loudspeaker and to pump up the volume, and, as he did that, we began to sing together at the top of our lungs, and I could hear our voices echoing through the square. "AM Israel Chai!" I felt a rush of joy I had never felt before. Here I was singing into the early German morning, jubilant in the knowledge that six million plus eleven angels hovered overhead eavesdropping on our every note, dancing in exultation.

Am Israel Chai!

The Mitzvah Van, recognizable around the world as Chabad's "Mitzvah Tank," is a large van operated by the Chabad Lubavitch organization as a mitzvah to the community; they provide education and guidance in the practice of Judaism, and they often provide transportation to the needy.